The History of the Quran

CRAFTED BY SKRIUWER

Copyright © 2025 by Skriuwer.

All rights reserved. No part of this book may be used or reproduced in any form whatsoever without written permission except in the case of brief quotations in critical articles or reviews.

At **Skriuwer**, we're more than just a team—we're a global community of people who love books. In Frisian, "Skriuwer" means "writer," and that's at the heart of what we do: creating and sharing books with readers worldwide. Wherever you are in the world, **Skriuwer** is here to inspire learning.

Frisian is one of the oldest languages in Europe, closely related to English and Dutch, and is spoken by about **500,000 people** in the province of **Friesland** (Fryslân), located in the northern Netherlands. It's the second official language of the Netherlands, but like many minority languages, Frisian faces the challenge of survival in a modern, globalized world.

We're using the money we earn to promote the Frisian language.

For more information, contact : **kontakt@skriuwer.com** (www.skriuwer.com)

TABLE OF CONTENTS

CHAPTER 1: ARABIA BEFORE ISLAM

- Socio-cultural setting in pre-Islamic Arabia
- Tribal alliances and the code of honor
- Religious plurality and the Ka'bah's role
- Significance of poetry and oral tradition

CHAPTER 2: THE EARLY LIFE OF PROPHET MUHAMMAD

- Lineage and upbringing in Mecca
- Influence of pre-Islamic social structures
- Early moral reputation (Al-Amin)
- Marriage to Khadijah and personal reflections

CHAPTER 3: THE FIRST REVELATIONS

- Night of Destiny in the Cave of Hira
- Initial fear and comfort from Khadijah
- Role of Waraqa ibn Nawfal in affirming prophethood
- Gradual resumption of revelation and early verses

CHAPTER 4: CHALLENGES AND GROWTH IN MECCA

- Public preaching and opposition by Quraysh
- Social boycotts and persecution
- Secret gatherings and clandestine conversion
- Early martyrs and the migration to Abyssinia

CHAPTER 5: MIGRATION TO MEDINA AND THE FORMATION OF A COMMUNITY

- Hijrah as a pivotal moment in Islamic history
- Establishing the Prophet's Mosque in Medina
- Brotherhood between the Muhajirun and the Ansar
- Constitution of Medina and social unity

CHAPTER 6: THE QURANIC REVELATIONS IN MEDINA

- Shift in tone: legislative and societal verses
- Guidance on warfare, treaties, and community ethics
- Evolution of Islamic rituals and worship
- Memorization and written records among the companions

CHAPTER 7: COMPILATION EFFORTS DURING THE PROPHET'S LIFETIME

- Recording on parchment, bones, and palm stalks
- Role of official scribes like Zayd ibn Thabit
- Annual review with Angel Jibril (especially in Ramadan)
- Ensuring accurate placement of newly revealed verses

CHAPTER 8: THE FAREWELL SERMON AND THE LAST REVELATIONS

- Hajj pilgrimage and final address to the ummah
- Core ethical directives in the Farewell Sermon
- Completion of revelation with the last verses
- Prophet Muhammad's passing and community grief

CHAPTER 9: THE PRESERVATION OF THE QURAN AFTER THE PROPHET'S DEATH

- *Immediate challenges and internal strife (Ridda Wars)*
- *Concerns over losing memorized portions*
- *Leadership transition: Abu Bakr's stewardship*
- *Scribal and memorization methods to maintain the text*

CHAPTER 10: CALIPH ABU BAKR'S ERA AND THE FIRST OFFICIAL COLLECTION

- *Initiation of the first compiled codex (Mushaf)*
- *Selection of Zayd ibn Thabit to lead the project*
- *Criteria of verification: witnesses and written fragments*
- *Outcome: a single recognized manuscript for the ummah*

CHAPTER 11: CALIPH UMAR'S PERIOD AND CONTINUED EXPANSION

- *Stabilizing the Islamic realm and administrative reforms*
- *Further spread of the Quran through new conquests*
- *Establishment of garrison towns (Kufa, Basra)*
- *Preservation of the Mushaf and uniform recitation traditions*

CHAPTER 12: CALIPH UTHMAN'S CANONIZATION AND DISTRIBUTION OF COPIES

- *Addressing dialectical variations in recitation*
- *Formation of an editorial committee under Zayd ibn Thabit*
- *Production of multiple official copies for key cities*
- *Instruction to destroy conflicting manuscripts*

CHAPTER 13: CALIPH ALI'S TIME AND EARLY QURANIC DEBATES

- Political turbulence and civil strife (Battle of the Camel, Siffin)
- Kharijite movement and their strict reading of the Quran
- Ali's deep knowledge and role in resolving interpretive disputes
- Ongoing unity around the Uthmanic Mushaf despite conflicts

CHAPTER 14: QURANIC MANUSCRIPTS AND EARLY ARABIC SCRIPTS

- Parchment, papyrus, and the codex format
- Development of Kufic and Hijazi scripts
- Introduction of diacritical marks and vowel notations
- Calligraphy and manuscript production under Umayyad patronage

---

CHAPTER 15: THE UMAYYAD PERIOD AND QURANIC DEVELOPMENTS

- Administrative unification and Arabic as official language
- Establishment of kuttab schools and mosque-based teaching
- Architectural expressions like the Dome of the Rock
- Basic diacritical systems to aid non-Arab communities

CHAPTER 16: THE ABBASID PERIOD AND RISE OF QURANIC SCHOLARSHIP

- Patronage of learning in Baghdad and House of Wisdom
- Formalizing grammar, qira'at, and tafsir methodology
- Major commentators like al-Tabari and advanced exegesis
- Debate over the Quran's nature (the Mihna) and theological schools

CHAPTER 17: MAJOR EARLY SCHOLARS OF THE QURAN

- Role of the Tabi'un in preserving companion teachings
- Influential figures like Ibn Abbas, Hasan al-Basri, and Mujahid
- Founders of recognized recitation lineages (Asim, Nafi', Ibn Kathir)
- Integration of grammar, philology, and exegesis

CHAPTER 18: TRANSMISSION ACROSS REGIONS AND CULTURES

- Spread into North Africa, al-Andalus, and Sub-Saharan Africa
- Dissemination through Persia, Central Asia, and the Indian subcontinent
- Southeast Asia and China: trade routes and Sufi missionaries
- Balancing universal Arabic recitation with local scripts and commentaries

CHAPTER 19: SCHOOLS OF RECITATION AND EARLY COMMENTARIES

- Canonical qira'at and criteria for authenticity
- Systematic teaching of oral recitation under master reciters
- Foundational tafsir methods: bi'l-ma'thur and bi'l-ra'y
- Interplay of variant readings and nuanced interpretation

CHAPTER 20: LASTING LEGACY IN EARLY ISLAMIC HISTORY

- Quran as the unifying scripture for diverse societies
- Influence on law, ethics, and governance
- Catalyst for linguistic, artistic, and intellectual flourishes
- Spiritual depth and continuity through memorization and study

Chapter One: Arabia Before Islam

1.1 Introduction to Pre-Islamic Arabia

Before the rise of Islam, Arabia was a land of diverse peoples, beliefs, and customs. It was not a unified country as we understand modern nations. Rather, it was a collection of tribes, clans, and small settlements scattered across a vast desert landscape. These communities were linked by shared language, common ancestry, and trade routes, but they often differed in religious practices, economic pursuits, and levels of social development.

Though many outside the region considered Arabia to be barren and isolated, it had an active cultural and economic life centered on important caravan routes. These routes allowed movement of goods, ideas, and customs from neighboring powers, such as the Byzantine Empire and the Sassanian Empire. This interchange of people and products made Arabia more cosmopolitan than often assumed, although local tribal traditions remained strong.

An essential part of understanding the history of the Quran is to appreciate this diverse backdrop. By knowing the setting in which Islam emerged, we gain a clearer view of the significance of its revelations, especially the profound impact those revelations had on Arabian society. In this chapter, we will examine the land, the people, the social structures, the prevailing religions, and the cultural norms that shaped Arabia in the centuries leading up to Islam.

1.2 The Geography of the Arabian Peninsula

Geographically, the Arabian Peninsula is surrounded by bodies of water on three sides: the Red Sea to the west, the Arabian Sea to the south, and the Persian Gulf to the east. To the north lie lands that connect to Greater Syria and Mesopotamia. Within this wide expanse, the climate varies, but large parts are dominated by harsh deserts, such as the Rub' al Khali (the Empty Quarter) and the Nafud Desert.

In the southwest region, where modern-day Yemen is located, the climate is more temperate compared to the interior. That area had been home to older and more complex civilizations that practiced terrace farming and built impressive irrigation systems. Central and northern Arabia were mostly desert plains inhabited by nomadic Bedouins or semi-nomadic tribes.

Water sources were primarily oases scattered throughout the desert. These oases could support date palms and some forms of agriculture. Around them, settlements grew as they served as stopping points for traveling caravans. Control of these water resources was a major factor in alliances, tribal power, and economic prosperity.

For travelers from Yemen or the eastern part of the peninsula heading toward Syria or Palestine, safe passage through these desert routes required local guidance and protection. Tribes made treaties with merchants and offered security in exchange for fees. Over time, certain towns became hubs for trade and gatherings, the most famous of which was Mecca.

1.3 Tribal Societies and Customs

1.3.1 Tribal Allegiance and Structure

Tribal identity was the core social unit for Arabs before Islam. Each tribe was made up of extended families that traced their lineage to a common ancestor. Loyalty within these tribes was paramount, and individuals relied on their tribe for protection and a sense of belonging. Conflicts between tribes often arose over resources, past grievances, or competition for trade opportunities.

In some areas, confederations of tribes formed to create larger groups, which sometimes led to the emergence of influential tribal leaders. However, no single political power controlled the entire peninsula. Instead, many tribes remained independent, governed by their own customs, traditions, and codes of honor.

1.3.2 The Code of Hospitality and Honor

Hospitality was, and remains, a significant virtue in Arab culture. Tribes prided themselves on being generous hosts. A traveler or stranger who arrived at a tent could expect a warm reception, food, and shelter. This code of hospitality was deeply embedded and reflected the harsh desert environment, where mutual assistance was crucial for survival.

Honor, or sharaf, was another central concept. For a tribe, honor depended on bravery, loyalty, the protection of weaker members, and the ability to uphold one's word. Reputation was critical, and many disputes could escalate quickly if a tribe's honor or a family's dignity was at stake. Such conflicts often resulted in feuds that could last generations unless resolved by negotiated settlements or arranged marriages between tribes.

1.3.3 Poetry and Oral Tradition

Poetry was highly respected and served as a form of storytelling, historical documentation, and cultural identity. Poets were valued as the voice of their tribes, preserving lineage histories, praises of tribal heroes, and laments for fallen warriors. Through verses, bards mocked enemies, praised allies, and expressed social values.

The Arabian Peninsula did not have widespread literacy, so oral tradition was the primary means of recording events, genealogies, and cultural norms. Poetic gatherings and competitions took place at markets and fairs, with the best poets gaining fame far beyond their homelands. The annual fair at Ukaz (near Mecca) was one such venue where poets, traders, and travelers gathered to compete, bargain, and share news.

1.4 Economics and Trade

1.4.1 Caravan Trade Routes

Trade was the lifeblood for many communities in Arabia. Caravans transported goods such as incense, spices, textiles, precious metals, and leather. Major routes connected the southern part of the peninsula (near Yemen and Hadramawt) to the northern regions bordering the Levant (Syria and Palestine). Another critical route ran from the Persian Gulf, carrying products from Mesopotamia and beyond.

These caravan routes were profitable but also treacherous. Bandits could attack unprotected caravans, so merchants often hired entire tribes or groups of armed guards. Though many inhabitants of Arabia engaged in small-scale farming or herding, trade provided opportunities to acquire wealth and goods from distant lands. It also exposed the people of Arabia to different cultures and religious ideas coming from neighboring empires.

1.4.2 Mecca as a Commercial Hub

Mecca, located in a mountainous region near the Red Sea, rose to importance due to its sanctuary, the Ka'bah, which was revered by various tribes. This religious significance contributed to Mecca becoming a safe zone where warring tribes would lay down their arms to conduct trade during pilgrimage seasons. The Quraysh tribe, which dominated Mecca, managed the trade caravans that traveled north and south. Over time, they grew wealthy and influential, establishing treaties with tribes along major routes to ensure protection of their merchandise.

Though Mecca was not as lush or agriculturally rich as other locations, its control over trade and its religious prominence made it pivotal in pre-Islamic Arabia. We will see how the rise of Islam intersected with this environment, as the Prophet Muhammad was born into the Quraysh tribe. But for now, it is important to note that Mecca's economic status influenced the region's politics and social dynamics.

1.5 Religions and Belief Systems

1.5.1 Polytheism and Idolatry

Before Islam, much of Arabia practiced a form of polytheism in which tribes worshiped various idols, deities, and nature spirits. Each tribe or region had its own set of gods, with Hubal, al-Lat, al-Uzza, and Manat being among the more famous. Many idols were kept inside or around the Ka'bah in Mecca, which was viewed as a sacred site even by pagans.

Pilgrimage to the Ka'bah was an established practice well before Islam, though it did not follow the rites that later became part of the Islamic Hajj. Instead, pre-Islamic Arabs performed certain rituals, circumambulated the Ka'bah, and honored their tribal gods. This pilgrimage season also drew trade from different regions, further boosting Mecca's economic stature.

1.5.2 Judaism and Christianity

Judaism had taken root in certain parts of Arabia, especially in Yemen and Yathrib (which would later be called Medina). Some Arab tribes had converted to

Judaism and upheld the Torah's traditions. In regions near modern-day Iraq or Greater Syria, Jewish communities had a notable presence, forming settlements that traded with their neighbors and sometimes intermarried with local Arab tribes.

Christianity had also spread to pockets of the peninsula, particularly in the north and the coastal regions with Byzantine influence. Monks, merchants, and Arab travelers who had contact with Christian territories brought elements of Christian faith and practice to the region. Churches existed in areas close to the borders of the Byzantine Empire. However, Christianity did not become the dominant religion in central Arabia.

1.5.3 Hanifism and Monotheistic Leanings

Some Arabs, known as Hanifs, rejected polytheism and idol worship in favor of a single God. They did not formally follow Jewish or Christian teachings; instead, they sought an original, pure monotheism akin to what they believed Abraham practiced. These individuals often spent time in solitude, reflecting on the nature of God and criticizing the pagan idol worship that surrounded them. Although they were few in number, their presence signaled a spiritual restlessness in pre-Islamic Arabia.

1.5.4 Religious Tolerance and Tensions

Despite the predominantly polytheistic environment, communities generally tolerated different faiths. Jews, Christians, and Hanifs often lived among polytheists. However, there was sometimes friction when it came to the supremacy of certain gods or the importance of tribal idols. Yet outright conflict over religious differences did not seem as widespread as tribal rivalries over resources or territory. More often, religion was one facet of tribal identity rather than the main cause of conflict.

1.6 Social and Cultural Practices

1.6.1 Marriage and Family

Marriages in pre-Islamic Arabia were often arranged to strengthen alliances between tribes. Polygamy was practiced, particularly by men of wealth or tribal leadership. Women's status varied: in some tribes, women held an esteemed position and could inherit wealth, manage property, and choose spouses. In others, cultural customs were stricter, and women had fewer rights. Some records indicate the practice of female infanticide when resources were scarce, though these practices varied widely and may not have been common to all tribes.

1.6.2 Slavery

Slavery was part of the social fabric. Both captured prisoners of war and individuals bought through trade became slaves. Slaves performed various tasks—some worked in agriculture, while others served as domestic workers in wealthier households. Conditions varied greatly, but in general, slaves had very limited rights and relied entirely on their owners. Freeing slaves was sometimes seen as an act of generosity, but there was no widespread movement to abolish slavery in pre-Islamic times.

1.6.3 Warfare and Raiding

Tribal feuds and raiding (ghazw) were a regular part of life. Raids could be a way to acquire resources, settle scores, or demonstrate tribal strength. When major conflicts erupted, alliances could form quickly, and battles often revolved around defending one's honor or retrieving stolen goods. Poetry and songs would later recount these conflicts, glorifying bravery and sacrifice.

1.6.4 Superstition and Omens

Many Arabs believed in jinn (invisible spirits) and sought to interpret omens through dreams, the flight patterns of birds, or other signs in nature. Fortune-tellers and soothsayers (kahins) played a role in guiding tribal decisions. Their pronouncements could shape important events like war, marriage alliances, or trade decisions. Yet, as we will see, Islam challenged many of these superstitious beliefs by emphasizing reliance on a single God.

1.7 Emergence of Poetry and Oral Tradition

1.7.1 The Role of Poets

Poets were the cultural celebrities of pre-Islamic Arabia. They functioned as historians, social critics, and spokespersons for their tribes. Through eloquent verse, they recounted significant events, praised tribal achievements, and mocked enemies. Poetic gatherings were occasions of excitement, and tribes competed to showcase their best poets. These competitions fostered creativity and sharpened the poetic tradition, setting the stage for a society that deeply appreciated the power of the spoken word.

1.7.2 The Seven Suspended Odes

One famous aspect of pre-Islamic poetry is the "Mu'allaqat," or the "Seven Suspended Odes." According to tradition, these were considered the finest examples of Arab poetry, hung on the walls of the Ka'bah in Mecca as a sign of great honor. Though modern scholars debate the details of this practice, the concept illustrates how revered poetry was in that society. These long poems touched on themes of love, heroism, tribal glory, and life in the desert.

1.7.3 Impact on Language Development

Arabic was already well-developed before Islam, but the prominence of poetry helped refine its vocabulary, style, and syntax. Poets played with complex meters, rhyme schemes, and figures of speech. This cultural emphasis on oral eloquence became a key part of Arab identity. When the Quran was later revealed, its poetic power and linguistic beauty made a strong impression, as it spoke in a language style that resonated with a society already attuned to the nuances of Arabic expression.

1.8 Key Regions: Mecca, Yathrib, Ta'if

1.8.1 Mecca

As noted, Mecca was a hub for both trade and religious gatherings. The Quraysh tribe held a prominent position there, managing the Ka'bah and hosting visitors during sacred months. Clashes were forbidden in the holy territory, making it a natural place to form deals and trade agreements. Mecca's economy benefited from these interactions, fueling the city's growth and the rise of influential families.

1.8.2 Yathrib (Medina)

North of Mecca lay Yathrib, a fertile oasis city that later became Medina. Multiple tribes resided there, including some Jewish communities that had settled in the region. Yathrib's agriculture, particularly date palm cultivation, played an important role in local prosperity. Tensions between local Arab tribes sometimes led to conflict, but the city's fertile land also offered a more settled way of life compared to desert nomadism.

1.8.3 Ta'if

Ta'if, located in the mountains east of Mecca, had a milder climate conducive to agriculture, including vineyards and orchards. It also held religious significance for certain tribes. Its strategic position along caravan routes made it a companion city to Mecca in trade terms. Although overshadowed by Mecca's prominence, Ta'if also boasted strong tribal aristocracy and wealth.

1.9 The Ka'bah and Religious Significance

The Ka'bah, a cube-shaped structure in the heart of Mecca, was revered even before Islam. Arab tradition held that it was established by the Prophet Abraham (Ibrahim) and his son Ishmael (Isma'il), though many local practices had strayed from the monotheism that Abraham preached. In pre-Islamic times, the Ka'bah housed numerous idols, with different tribes placing their own within its walls.

The custodianship of the Ka'bah was highly coveted, as it brought social prestige and economic gain. People would travel to Mecca during certain months for pilgrimage, generating income for local merchants and caravan leaders. Over time, the Ka'bah's sacred status became deeply woven into the identity of the Arabian tribes, making Mecca a natural center for gatherings.

Chapter Two: The Early Life of Prophet Muhammad

2.1 Introduction

Prophet Muhammad's early life took place within the dynamic setting of Mecca, a city that was both a commercial center and a major religious site. Born into the Quraysh tribe, he experienced firsthand the cultural and economic fabric of Arabia. Though Islam had not yet appeared on the scene, his upbringing reflected the values, tensions, and customs that shaped pre-Islamic society.

In this chapter, we will discuss the Prophet's genealogy, childhood, guardianship, early work experiences, and marriage. We will also look at Meccan society through his eyes, seeing how his character developed and how he became recognized as a person of trust and integrity. This background sets the stage for the momentous events that follow in his life—events that forever changed the course of Arabia and the wider world.

2.2 The Genealogy of Prophet Muhammad

2.2.1 Lineage within the Quraysh Tribe

Prophet Muhammad was born in 570 CE (approximate date; some sources give 571 CE) to a family belonging to the Hashim clan of the Quraysh tribe. The Quraysh were the guardians of the Ka'bah and influential in Meccan trade. His lineage is traced back to Adnan, and Islamic tradition ultimately connects it to the Prophet Ishmael, the son of Abraham. This genealogical connection was deeply respected in Mecca, as descent from Ishmael was a mark of nobility among Arabs.

The Hashim clan itself was known for its role in feeding and providing water to pilgrims who came to Mecca. Muhammad's grandfather, Abd al-Muttalib, was a well-respected leader who handled many of the affairs related to the Ka'bah. He was known for rediscovering the Zamzam well, an important water source near the Ka'bah that had been lost for some time.

2.2.2 The Parents: Abdullah and Aminah

Muhammad's father, Abdullah, was the son of Abd al-Muttalib. He married Aminah bint Wahb, a woman from the Zahrah clan, also part of the Quraysh network. Abdullah died when Aminah was pregnant with Muhammad, leaving the newborn without a father from birth. This loss affected Muhammad's social standing, as having a living father was significant in tribal society. However, because of Abd al-Muttalib's status, the child still had important familial support.

Aminah was known for her honorable character. Though little is recorded about her personal life, later Islamic sources highlight that she had dreams or signs indicating the significance of the child she carried. She passed away when Muhammad was around six years old, leaving him an orphan at a very young age.

2.3 Birth and Early Childhood

2.3.1 Birth in Mecca

Muhammad's birth, according to most accounts, occurred in the year called the "Year of the Elephant," referencing an attempted invasion of Mecca by the Abyssinian ruler Abraha, who brought war elephants to attack the Ka'bah. This event became part of Meccan lore, marking a significant year in local memory. The precise date of his birth is debated, with some citing Rabi' al-Awwal (the third month of the Islamic calendar).

Though the region was often unstable, the people of Mecca took pride in surviving such threats. The birth of Muhammad into the Hashim clan came at a time when the Quraysh were increasing in wealth and influence through caravan trade.

2.3.2 Foster Care in the Desert

It was customary in Mecca for infants to be sent to live with Bedouin tribes in the countryside. This practice aimed to strengthen the child's body and immerse them in the pure Arabic language, away from the distractions of city life. Muhammad was entrusted to Halimah bint Abi Dhu'ayb, from the Sa'd ibn Bakr tribe.

Halimah's household was initially marked by poverty, but they reportedly experienced blessings in their livelihood while caring for Muhammad. These anecdotes shaped the popular image of Muhammad even from infancy—namely, that he brought blessings to those around him. Muhammad stayed with Halimah's family until he was about four or five years old, after which he returned to Mecca.

2.3.3 Return to Aminah and Loss of a Mother

Upon returning, Muhammad lived under the care of his mother, Aminah, for a short period. She decided to take him on a journey to Yathrib (Medina) to visit his maternal relatives. During or soon after this trip, Aminah fell ill and passed away. Losing his mother at the age of six made Muhammad a complete orphan, dependent on his grandfather and, later, on his uncle for guidance and care.

2.4 The Care of Abd al-Muttalib and Abu Talib

2.4.1 Life Under Grandfather Abd al-Muttalib

After Aminah's death, Muhammad's grandfather, Abd al-Muttalib, took him in. Abd al-Muttalib was advanced in age but deeply loved his orphaned grandson. He recognized something special in the child, sometimes seating him close to where he conducted tribal discussions. This gave Muhammad a glimpse into leadership and decision-making processes.

However, Abd al-Muttalib died when Muhammad was eight years old. Despite the short time they shared, the grandfather's affection and concern for Muhammad left a lasting impression. Through these experiences, Muhammad learned about tribal leadership, local politics, and the significance of the Ka'bah.

2.4.2 Guardianship Under Abu Talib

Leadership of the Hashim clan passed to Abu Talib, one of Abd al-Muttalib's sons and Muhammad's uncle. Abu Talib was a respected figure in Mecca, though not among the wealthiest. He took responsibility for Muhammad, raising him alongside his own children. Muhammad shared household duties and developed close bonds with his cousins, especially Ali ibn Abi Talib, who would later play a major role in Islamic history.

Abu Talib's guardianship was crucial, as he introduced Muhammad to the caravan trade. From a young age, Muhammad accompanied his uncle on trading journeys to Syria, observing the culture of commerce, dealing, and negotiation. These trips exposed him to a broader world beyond Mecca, possibly including encounters with Jewish and Christian communities along the trade routes.

2.5 Adulthood: Merchant Activities and Reputation

2.5.1 The Title Al-Amin (The Trustworthy)

As Muhammad grew, he gained a reputation for honesty and integrity. He was widely known as "Al-Amin," meaning "the trustworthy one." This was no small feat in a society where tribal conflicts and shifting alliances often bred suspicion. People in Mecca turned to him for help in settling disputes, keeping valuables, and mediating disagreements because they recognized that he dealt fairly with everyone.

2.5.2 Early Work Experiences

Besides the caravans, Muhammad may have engaged in various small trading initiatives to support himself and his uncle's family. In Meccan society, success in trade required negotiation skills, reliability, and a sense of fairness. Muhammad's upright dealings set him apart, and word of his integrity spread.

It is during this stage of his life that we see the beginnings of the qualities that would define him as a prophet—his sense of justice, compassion, and commitment to truthful conduct. People respected him not for wealth or power, but for the moral character that shone through his everyday actions.

2.5.3 Encounter with Monk Bahira (Traditional Narration)

Some Islamic traditions mention that during one of these trade journeys to Syria, a Christian monk named Bahira recognized signs of prophethood in the young Muhammad. The story says that Bahira advised Abu Talib to protect the boy, warning that some people might try to harm him if they recognized his future importance. While this account is considered part of Islamic legend and is not confirmed by every historical source, it highlights the belief that Muhammad's destiny as a prophet was discernible even in his youth.

2.6 Marriage to Khadijah and Family Life

2.6.1 Khadijah's Background

Khadijah bint Khuwaylid was a wealthy and successful merchant in Mecca. Born into a noble family from the Quraysh, she inherited her late husband's business and managed trade caravans. She was respected for her intelligence, leadership, and strong moral character. At a time when women were not always granted authority, Khadijah stood out as a self-assured figure in Meccan commerce.

2.6.2 Proposal and Marriage

Hearing about Muhammad's honesty and skill in trade, Khadijah hired him to lead one of her caravans to Syria. The venture proved profitable, and upon his return, Muhammad gave a thorough and honest account of the trade. Impressed by his character, Khadijah proposed marriage to him, despite being around 40 years old while Muhammad was about 25.

Their marriage was harmonious. According to Islamic tradition, Khadijah provided emotional and financial stability, allowing Muhammad to continue his contemplative nature. She was the first person to believe in his prophethood years later, supporting him when few others did. Their union produced several children, although only four daughters—Zainab, Ruqayyah, Umm Kulthum, and Fatimah—survived to adulthood.

2.6.3 Significance of This Relationship

The marriage to Khadijah elevated Muhammad's social and economic standing. He no longer struggled financially, which granted him more freedom to spend time in reflection and service to the community. Khadijah's unwavering support proved to be a cornerstone of his future mission. Historically, their partnership is often viewed as a prime example of marital harmony, shared purpose, and deep mutual respect.

2.7 Reflections on Meccan Society

2.7.1 Inequalities and Tribal Hierarchies

Though Muhammad was part of a reputable clan, he witnessed how power was unevenly distributed in Mecca. Wealthy traders, particularly among the Quraysh elite, could influence the city's politics and economy. The poor, orphans, and slaves had limited recourse if they were mistreated. Tribal affiliations also shaped social status, and an individual without strong connections faced marginalization.

2.7.2 The Presence of Idols in the Ka'bah

Muhammad walked past the Ka'bah every day, observing the numerous idols that each tribe placed in the sanctuary. Growing up, he likely saw the rituals performed by idol-worshipers and questioned their validity. Though not much is recorded about his early religious inclinations, later developments suggest he had no trust in idols and felt drawn to the concept of one God.

2.7.3 Moral and Spiritual Questions

By the time he reached adulthood, Muhammad was known for his introspective nature. While people attended social gatherings and worshiped idols, he sought solitude and quiet spaces away from the bustle. This reflective approach led him to contemplate the deeper moral questions of life, the fate of the oppressed, and the ultimate purpose behind existence. His experiences with orphans, poor travelers, and downtrodden individuals may have moved him to think about social justice long before he became a prophet.

2.8 The Hilf al-Fudul (Alliance of the Virtuous)

2.8.1 Formation of an Ethical Pact

One noteworthy event during Muhammad's youth was the "Hilf al-Fudul," a pact made by certain Meccan leaders to protect the rights of the vulnerable, ensure fair trade, and stand against injustice. This alliance formed when a merchant was wronged by a member of a powerful clan, and no one would stand up for him. Moved by outrage over this injustice, several individuals from various tribes gathered to pledge that they would collectively protect anyone who was oppressed, regardless of tribal affiliation.

2.8.2 Muhammad's Participation

Though young, Muhammad took part in this pact. It resonated with his sense of fairness and compassion for the weak. In later years, he would reflect on the Hilf al-Fudul, remarking that he would participate in such a pact again if given the chance. This shows how early experiences formed the moral bedrock from which Islam's message of justice and compassion would later emerge.

2.9 The Prophet's Character: Al-Sadiq (The Truthful) and Al-Amin (The Trustworthy)

2.9.1 A Reputation for Honesty

Muhammad's peers knew him as someone who never engaged in deceitful practices common among some merchants of that era. He avoided lying, cheating, or taking advantage of others. This is crucial background because once he started preaching the message of Islam, people could not easily accuse him of dishonesty; his personal record spoke for itself.

2.9.2 Modesty and Humility

Despite his respected status and the wealth provided by marriage to Khadijah, Muhammad maintained a modest lifestyle. He was generous to the less fortunate and upheld strong ethical behavior. He did not indulge in excesses or show arrogance toward others. This humility stood in contrast to some wealthy clans that flaunted their riches.

2.9.3 Compassion Toward the Weak

Accounts from this period describe his kindness toward the poor, slaves, and orphans, likely influenced by his own experiences as an orphan. He empathized with those who lacked tribal protection. This empathy set him apart from many of his contemporaries, who often saw social hierarchies as fixed and cared primarily for the interests of their own clans.

2.10 The Stage Set for Revelation

2.10.1 Solitude in the Cave of Hira

As Muhammad approached his late thirties, his habit of retreating to the Cave of Hira on Mount Nur near Mecca became a regular practice. There, he spent nights in contemplation, prayer, and fasting, though the exact form of his devotion differed from the established pagan rituals. He sought refuge from the noise of the city and the moral issues he observed, looking for higher meaning and guidance.

2.10.2 Disconnect from Idolatry

No records suggest that Muhammad took part in idol worship. Although he did not openly challenge the system yet, his personal life seemed guided by a monotheistic inclination, reminiscent of the Hanifs who professed belief in one God. Khadijah supported him, providing him provisions for his solitary retreats. It was during one of these periods of isolation that his life—and the course of Meccan society—would change forever.

2.10.3 Path Toward Prophethood

Muhammad's early life experiences—his orphanhood, his guardianship under his uncle, his reputation for honesty, his marriage to a supportive wife, and his concern for the less fortunate—formed a moral and emotional foundation. This foundation prepared him to receive a revelation that would not only transform him but also bring profound change to Arabia. By the end of his second decade of adulthood, he had seen enough of Meccan society to recognize its faults and yearn for something more meaningful.

In the next chapters, we will detail how the revelation of the Quran began, how Muhammad reacted to it, and how the people around him received this new message. These pivotal events launch the Islamic faith and set in motion changes that would eventually reshape the Arabian Peninsula from within.

Chapter Three: The First Revelations

3.1 Introduction

By the end of his youth, Muhammad had developed a habit of retreating to the Cave of Hira, located on the outskirts of Mecca. He sought solitude to ponder life's deeper questions, away from the daily bustle of the city and the practice of idol worship that surrounded him. His concerns included the inequality he witnessed in Meccan society, the plight of orphans and the poor, and the worship of multiple idols in and around the Ka'bah. These reflections set the stage for a life-altering event: the beginning of the Quranic revelations.

This chapter explores the moment of the first revelation, the immediate emotional and spiritual impact it had on Muhammad, and the earliest responses from those close to him. We will look at the progression of revelations, the nature of the early Quranic verses, and how these messages guided the small community of new believers in the initial days of Islam.

3.2 The Cave of Hira

3.2.1 Muhammad's Retreats to the Mountain

Located about three miles from the center of Mecca, the Cave of Hira sits on the rocky slopes of a mountain known as Jabal al-Nur (the Mountain of Light). It is not large, but it offered enough space for a person to sit or stand in prayer, looking over the wide horizon. From the entrance, one can see parts of Mecca below.

Tradition holds that Muhammad would spend many nights there, sometimes taking enough provisions to remain in solitude for extended periods. He would reflect on life, question the status quo, and contemplate the nature of the Creator. At this stage, he did not publicly declare himself to follow a specific religious system, but he leaned toward monotheism, rejecting idolatry. In these quiet moments, he found calmness that contrasted with the restless environment of Mecca.

3.2.2 Night of Destiny

It was during one of these retreats, specifically during the Islamic month of Ramadan (though Islam as an institution had not yet formed, later Muslim tradition associates the event with Ramadan), that Muhammad encountered something extraordinary. He was around forty years old—an age by which a person in Arabian society was considered mature and wise. It was here, according to the vast majority of Islamic sources, that the Angel Jibril (Gabriel) visited him for the first time to deliver the divine message.

3.3 The First Revelation

3.3.1 Angelic Appearance

Muhammad was in the cave when he sensed the presence of another being. He later described that he was suddenly gripped by a force that pressed upon him and a commanding voice said, "Read!" (or "Recite!"). Feeling unable to read or recite anything unknown to him, Muhammad responded that he was not learned or could not read. The voice repeated the command and pressed upon him again, releasing him after a moment. Then the angel recited words that would become the opening verses of Surah al-Alaq (chapter 96 of the Quran):

> "Read in the name of your Lord who created,
> Created man from a clinging form.
> Read, and your Lord is the Most Generous,
> Who taught by the pen,
> Taught man what he did not know."

These lines stress knowledge, the act of reading, and recognizing God as the creator and teacher of humankind. They form the very first revelation that set Islam into motion.

3.3.2 Muhammad's Reaction

The experience left Muhammad shaken and filled with fear. He had not experienced anything like it before. Tradition describes him fleeing the cave and descending the mountain, heart pounding, unsure of the nature of this encounter. Unlike a dream or a typical vision, this event felt intensely physical and real. He worried about his sanity, fearing a supernatural encounter that might be harmful or a sign that he had lost his mind.

He rushed home to Khadijah, his wife, and asked her to cover him with a blanket. He told her, "Cover me, cover me," seeking comfort and protection. His body trembled, and his heart pounded as he recalled the angel's command. This overwhelming emotion gives us insight into the human side of the prophet-to-be, showing that he did not expect or immediately embrace this newfound responsibility. Instead, he felt deep apprehension.

3.4 Khadijah's Support and Waraqa ibn Nawfal

3.4.1 Khadijah's Reassurance

Khadijah played a crucial role in calming him down, affirming the goodness she saw in his character. She assured him that God would not disgrace someone who was known for truthfulness, caring for the poor and needy, and showing hospitality to guests. Her words reflect the moral qualities that made Muhammad so respected in Mecca, even before the revelation.

Khadijah did not doubt him. Instead, she offered immediate support. She saw sincerity in his fear, recognized the possibility that this event was from a higher power, and sought to find further clarification on what had happened. Her reaction laid the foundation of faith in Muhammad's mission.

3.4.2 Consultation with Waraqa ibn Nawfal

Khadijah decided to visit her elderly cousin, Waraqa ibn Nawfal, who was known to be a monotheist. He was familiar with religious scriptures, possibly having studied parts of the Torah and the Gospel. Waraqa listened carefully to Muhammad's account of the angelic visitation.

Upon hearing the details, Waraqa declared that the visitor was indeed the Angel Gabriel, the same angel said to have come to earlier prophets. He added that if he (Waraqa) were younger and lived until Muhammad was driven out of Mecca, he would stand by him. Waraqa recognized the pattern of prophethood and the hardships prophets faced when preaching a message that opposed popular beliefs and idol worship.

This meeting comforted Muhammad, but it also hinted at the trials he would face. Waraqa predicted that people would oppose him once he began to share the revelation publicly. Still, at this earliest stage, Muhammad did not fully grasp the extent of what lay ahead.

3.5 Initial Pause and Subsequent Revelations

3.5.1 The Interruption (Fatrah)

Islamic tradition mentions a period known as the "fatrah," a gap where revelation temporarily ceased after the initial verses of Surah al-Alaq. The length of this pause is debated in different historical accounts—some say it lasted for days, others for months. During this time, Muhammad felt anxiety and longing. He wondered whether the angel would return or if God had chosen someone else.

This pause served as a test of patience and faith. It gave Muhammad the opportunity to reflect on the first revelation, to gather his thoughts, and to slowly accept the enormity of the mission. Khadijah remained by his side, offering reassurance and emotional support.

3.5.2 Revelation Resumes

Then, one day, while Muhammad was walking, the angel appeared again, filling the sky and proclaiming that he was indeed Gabriel. Some accounts say that Muhammad felt an overwhelming presence that removed his doubts. The angel revealed more verses, reinforcing the message that Muhammad was chosen to deliver God's word.

Among the early revelations after Surah al-Alaq were verses from Surah al-Muddaththir (chapter 74), where Muhammad is addressed as "O you wrapped up (in garments)." He is commanded to arise and warn people, to magnify his Lord, to purify himself, and to shun idols. This passage carries a tone of urgency and outlines the tasks ahead: proclaiming the message, focusing on God's greatness, and avoiding the corrupt practices of idolatry.

3.6 Early Themes of the Revelations

3.6.1 Monotheism

A core theme in these first revelations was the oneness of God (tawhid). In a society where multiple idols were worshiped, the Quran asserted that there is only one Creator, deserving of worship and reliance. This message stood in contrast to the dominant religious practices of Mecca, where the Ka'bah housed numerous tribal idols.

3.6.2 Moral Uprightness and Social Justice

Another significant focus of the early revelations was moral uprightness. The Quran called for honesty, caring for the poor, and upholding justice. These ideas struck at the heart of Meccan society, which had stark divisions between the wealthy elite and the marginalized. Muhammad's personal conduct already exemplified many of these virtues, giving credibility to his preaching.

3.6.3 Emphasis on Knowledge

From the very first word revealed—"Read!"—the Quran placed a strong emphasis on knowledge, learning, and understanding. This was a transformative idea in a largely oral culture. The revelations invited reflection on the natural world, history, and human relationships, urging people to seek truth and wisdom.

3.6.4 Warning and Hope

Early Quranic passages offered both warnings and messages of hope. They warned of God's judgment for those who persist in wrongdoing and reminded listeners of past communities who turned away from divine guidance. Yet they also promised mercy and forgiveness for those who repent and lead righteous lives. This balance of warning and hope underscored the moral accountability that the Quran introduced.

3.7 The First Believers

3.7.1 Khadijah, the First Muslim

Khadijah is widely recognized as the first person to accept Muhammad's prophethood. Her unwavering trust, along with her knowledge of his character, allowed her to embrace the message without hesitation. She remained his most loyal supporter in the early days, using her influence and resources to protect the small community of believers.

3.7.2 Ali ibn Abi Talib

Ali was Muhammad's young cousin, living under his care in Abu Talib's household. Accounts say that Ali accepted Islam at a very early age, possibly around ten. Though a child, Ali's acceptance symbolized the close familial bond and trust in Muhammad's integrity. Ali would eventually become a major figure in Islamic history, but during these initial revelations, he quietly followed his cousin's teachings.

3.7.3 Zayd ibn Harithah

Zayd was once a slave who later became an adopted son of Muhammad. After witnessing Muhammad's life and the message he was preaching, Zayd embraced Islam wholeheartedly. His devotion and loyalty were well-known, reflecting the appeal the new faith had for those marginalized by tribal structures.

3.7.4 Abu Bakr as-Siddiq

Abu Bakr was an influential merchant and close friend of Muhammad. Known for his gentle manner and trustworthy reputation, Abu Bakr became one of the earliest converts. His acceptance led to other notable figures, such as Uthman ibn Affan and Sa'd ibn Abi Waqqas, joining the faith. Abu Bakr's wealth and social standing helped protect the growing movement in its infancy.

3.8 Secretive Preaching

3.8.1 The House of al-Arqam

For the first few years, the message of Islam was spread discreetly. Muhammad and his small group of followers met in private homes to study and pray together. One such place was the house of al-Arqam near the foot of the Safa hill in Mecca. This allowed new Muslims to learn about their faith away from public scrutiny and potential hostility.

3.8.2 Gradual Growth

During this secret phase, the community expanded slowly but steadily. People were attracted by the call to worship one God and the ethical teachings that championed honesty, compassion, and unity. The teachings also appealed to those who felt oppressed or disillusioned by existing tribal hierarchies. Converts spanned different backgrounds: some were wealthy traders, some were slaves, and others were from middle-class families.

3.8.3 Risk of Persecution

Though public opposition had not yet become violent, the small group remained cautious. In tribal Mecca, any deviation from established customs could provoke anger. The idol-worshiping elite, benefiting from the status quo, would not welcome a message that dismissed their deities and threatened their lucrative pilgrimage business. Muhammad and his followers prepared for the possibility of backlash, though the intensity of future hostilities was still unknown.

3.9 Early Forms of Worship and Ritual

3.9.1 Prayer (Salah)

Even during the secret period, prayer was a key component of the new faith. The exact form of the five daily prayers had not yet been fully established, but believers would stand, bow, and prostrate in devotion to the one God. Muhammad taught them simple supplications and verses from the Quran that had been revealed. This act of communal worship set them apart from their fellow Meccans, who bowed and prayed before idols.

3.9.2 Moral Conduct

The revelations encouraged righteous behavior, honesty in trade, kindness to neighbors, and assistance to the needy. Although the legal injunctions we now associate with Islam (like specific regulations for fasting, almsgiving, and pilgrimage) would come later, the emphasis on moral conduct was already present. Muslims strove to avoid fraud, exploitation, and other common misdeeds.

3.9.3 Recitation of the Revealed Verses

Reciting the Quranic verses among themselves became a distinct form of worship. Since most people did not read and write, memorization was crucial. Hearing the melodious language of the Quran in small gatherings profoundly affected listeners, drawing them closer to the faith. This oral transmission also served as an important means of preserving the revealed text before any official written compilation existed.

3.10 Shift to Public Preaching

3.10.1 Command to Preach Openly

After a period of private teaching, Muhammad received a revelation instructing him to proclaim the message openly. One often-cited verse related to this shift is from Surah al-Hijr (15:94): "Therefore proclaim openly what you have been commanded, and turn away from the polytheists." This directive brought a new phase: no longer would the message be contained within small, secret circles.

3.10.2 Invitation to Clan Members

Muhammad began by inviting his own relatives to abandon idolatry and worship God alone. He called together members of the Hashim clan and warned them of the consequences of ignoring divine guidance. Some, like his uncle Abu Lahab, opposed him fiercely. Others, like Abu Talib, chose to protect Muhammad out of family loyalty, even if they did not fully accept the new faith.

3.10.3 Climbing Mount Safa

A famous account narrates that Muhammad once climbed Mount Safa, a small hill near the Ka'bah, and called out to the Quraysh. When they gathered, expecting important news (as a warning from a trustworthy man was taken seriously), Muhammad declared his prophethood and told them of God's oneness. Abu Lahab responded angrily, rejecting him in harsh terms. This public declaration solidified the shift from quiet gatherings to a more confrontational stance with the idol-worshiping majority.

3.11 Initial Reaction from Mecca

3.11.1 Curiosity, Skepticism, and Hostility

The people of Mecca received Muhammad's message with a mixture of curiosity and skepticism. Some were intrigued by the idea of a single God, especially if they had encountered monotheistic traditions through trade or local Christian and Jewish contacts. Others saw the new faith as a threat to the established order, endangering the pilgrimage trade tied to the Ka'bah's idols.

Leaders of the Quraysh who profited from idol worship viewed Muhammad's call as subversive. He condemned many of their practices, from fraudulent trading to neglecting the poor. If his popularity grew, they feared losing both economic benefits and social control.

3.11.2 Tactics of Pressure

At first, the leaders of the Quraysh tried to reason with Muhammad, offering him wealth or status if he would abandon his teachings. When he refused, they resorted to ridicule—accusing him of being a poet, a soothsayer, or someone possessed by spirits. They demanded miraculous signs, mocking the fact that they could see no immediate physical wonders aside from the words of the Quran.

3.11.3 Emergence of Hostility

Though not yet at its peak, hostility began to grow. Some of the new Muslims from weaker tribes or who were slaves faced insults or minor harassment. The stage was being set for more severe persecution, especially as Islam continued to gain followers. Despite these pressures, Muhammad did not waver in sharing the revelations he continued to receive.

3.12 Significance of the Early Revelations

3.12.1 Establishing the Concept of Prophethood

These initial revelations highlighted the role of Muhammad as a messenger transmitting God's words. Unlike a poet drawing on personal inspiration, he claimed no authorship over the Quran. This marked a clear distinction in how Meccans viewed him: he was not merely a wise man but a conduit for divine speech.

3.12.2 Foundations of Islamic Theology

The earliest chapters laid the foundations of Islamic theology: belief in one God, acceptance of Muhammad as His messenger, and the concept of accountability in the hereafter. They also emphasized God's mercy and compassion, underscoring that faith and righteous actions lead to forgiveness and salvation.

3.12.3 Moral and Social Reform

These revelations challenged the social norms of Mecca by calling for fairness in commerce, just treatment of the poor, and the rejection of idol worship. The intensity of the moral and social reform message set Islam apart. It was not a mere personal spiritual path but a collective call to transform society.

3.13 Personal Trials of the Prophet

3.13.1 Emotional Weight

Receiving the Quranic revelations was both a spiritual honor and a heavy responsibility. Muhammad felt the weight of this burden acutely. Some accounts describe physical discomfort or sweating when revelations descended, indicating the profound nature of the experience. Mentally, he carried the knowledge that many of his own tribespeople would reject his call and possibly turn against him.

3.13.2 Dependence on Divine Guidance

During these early days, the Prophet's dependence on divine guidance grew stronger. Verses comforted him, reassured him of God's support, and instructed him on how to deal with critics. In the face of increasing opposition, these messages fortified his resolve. The Quran itself served as a living source of moral and spiritual strength for him and the small community of believers.

3.13.3 The Importance of Khadijah

Khadijah remained a pillar of emotional support. She used her resources to ease the burdens that came with preaching. Her home served as a haven for those exploring Islam, and her encouragement was vital at times when outside hostility felt overwhelming. The bond between them exemplified how critical supportive relationships can be during periods of social upheaval.

3.14 Lessons from the Earliest Surahs

3.14.1 Surah Al-Fatiha

Though scholars debate precisely when Surah Al-Fatiha (the Opening) was fully revealed, it is often considered an early chapter. It is a short but comprehensive prayer that praises God's mercy, affirms His sovereignty over the Day of Judgment, and requests guidance on the straight path. This surah quickly became central to Muslim prayer.

3.14.2 Surah Al-Muzzammil and Surah Al-Muddaththir

These chapters, also from the early period, instruct Muhammad to stand in prayer at night, to purify his garments, and to spread the message despite opposition. They reiterate themes of dedication, spiritual discipline, and reliance on God. Their style is urgent, reflecting the pivotal nature of establishing a new faith community.

3.14.3 Surah Ad-Duha and Surah Al-Inshirah

Additional short surahs addressed Muhammad's concerns, promising that God had not forsaken him. Surah Ad-Duha (93) speaks of God's care for the orphan and the needy, reminding Muhammad of how he was guided and protected in his own life. Surah Al-Inshirah (94) reassures him that ease will follow hardship, an encouragement that future trials would not last forever.

3.15 The Broader Context of Revelation

3.15.1 Oral Culture

In a predominantly oral society, the beauty and rhythm of the Quran's verses commanded attention. Skilled poets existed in Mecca, but the Quran's style was neither poetry nor prose. It had a unique cadence that drew listeners in, even if they initially disagreed with the message. This literary power played a crucial role in the spread of Islam, as people memorized entire passages after hearing them recited.

3.15.2 Preservation by Memorization

Before any systematic written compilation, new verses were memorized by those who heard them first. Muhammad would recite them to his followers, who repeated them until they knew them by heart. Trusted scribes also wrote down verses on available materials like parchment, bones, and palm leaves. Thus, a blend of oral and written methods began preserving the Quran from the earliest days.

3.15.3 Gradual Revelation

Instead of revealing the Quran all at once, God sent it down in portions over about twenty-three years. This gradual approach helped the believers internalize teachings step by step, addressing unfolding situations in Mecca and later in Medina. It also allowed for immediate guidance when urgent matters arose, such as questions of communal ethics or handling opposition.

Chapter Four: Challenges and Growth in Mecca

4.1 Introduction

Once Muhammad was commanded to proclaim the message of Islam openly, the atmosphere in Mecca began to shift. In the early secret phase, the Quraysh leaders knew little about the small gatherings taking place in private homes. But when Muhammad stood on Mount Safa to deliver the core message—worship one God and shun idols—he touched the city's economic, social, and cultural foundations. The Ka'bah was central to Mecca's lucrative pilgrimage business, and idol worship had deep tribal roots.

This chapter explores the mounting challenges faced by Muhammad and his followers as they called people to Islam in a city resistant to change. It covers the Quraysh's tactics, from mockery and social pressure to outright persecution, and details how the small community responded. Despite oppression, Islam grew in numbers and in moral strength, attracting individuals from diverse backgrounds. By understanding this critical period, we see how the Quran's revelations and the Prophet's leadership helped unify and fortify the nascent Muslim community under increasing external threats.

4.2 Mecca's Initial Response to Open Preaching

4.2.1 Indifference and Curiosity

When Muhammad first publicly declared his mission, some Meccans responded with indifference. They saw him as another figure with personal religious ideas, hardly a direct threat. Others were curious, especially when they heard recitations of the Quran. They noticed its linguistic beauty and the boldness of its monotheistic claim. Small pockets of people began to whisper: "What is he saying? Could this be true?"

4.2.2 Growing Concern Among the Quraysh Leaders

However, influential members of the Quraysh, including Abu Sufyan, Abu Jahl, and Abu Lahab, quickly grew alarmed. They recognized that if Muhammad's message took hold, it would undermine idol worship. Pilgrims who came to honor their tribal gods might abandon Mecca's idols, hurting local commerce. Worse, the social order that privileged the wealthy clans could be disrupted by a faith that stressed equality and charity toward the poor.

They also feared that the new faith would damage Mecca's alliances with other tribes. Mutual respect among tribes sometimes hinged on each tribe's idol or deity placed around the Ka'bah. If Muhammad dismissed all idols, outside tribes could break ties with Mecca. Quraysh leaders thus saw Islam not just as a religious issue but as a societal threat.

4.3 Methods of Opposition

4.3.1 Ridicule and Slander

One of the first strategies the Quraysh employed was ridicule. They accused Muhammad of being a madman, a poet, or someone possessed by jinn (invisible spirits). This name-calling aimed to damage his credibility, especially since the Arabs valued mental clarity and shunned the idea of madness or possession.

Additionally, they twisted his words to cast doubt. When Muhammad spoke of resurrection and the Day of Judgment, some mocked by asking how bones long turned to dust could be brought back to life. The Quran records some of these taunts and counters them by emphasizing God's power to create life from nothing, let alone resurrect it.

4.3.2 Trying to Bargain

Leaders like Utbah ibn Rabi'ah approached Muhammad with offers to stop his preaching. They promised wealth, marriage to any woman of his choice, or high political status if he would remain silent. Muhammad declined these offers, reciting verses from the Quran that underscored his mission's divine mandate. His refusal highlighted that he was not motivated by material gain or personal power.

4.3.3 Family Pressure

Tribal society in Mecca placed great emphasis on family and clan loyalty. The Quraysh pressured Abu Talib, Muhammad's uncle and protector, to convince his nephew to abandon his message. While Abu Talib did not convert to Islam, he defended Muhammad out of family duty. This put Abu Talib in a difficult position—balancing tribal expectations with loyalty to his nephew.

4.3.4 Escalation to Persecution

When persuasion and bargaining failed, some Quraysh leaders escalated their tactics. They focused on vulnerable Muslims—particularly those without influential tribal backing. Slaves or former slaves who converted, like Bilal ibn Rabah, faced brutal punishments. Bilal was dragged in the scorching desert and whipped, told to renounce Islam. He famously persisted in proclaiming God's oneness, highlighting the early Muslims' steadfast belief.

Others were forced to endure hunger, physical torture, and social isolation. This strategy aimed to deter new converts. If the punishment for believing Muhammad's message was severe, fewer people might risk joining him.

4.4 Notable Early Converts and Persecutions

4.4.1 Sumayyah bint Khayyat and Yasir

Sumayyah and her husband Yasir were among the earliest Muslim families to suffer. They belonged to a less powerful background, lacking a strong clan to shield them. The Quraysh tormented them publicly to set an example. Sumayyah, considered by Islamic tradition as the first female martyr of Islam, was killed for refusing to renounce her faith. Her steadfastness became an inspiration for generations of Muslims to come, symbolizing courage in the face of oppression.

4.4.2 Bilal ibn Rabah

Bilal's story is one of resilience. Originally from Abyssinia (Ethiopia), he served as a slave in Mecca. After converting, he was subjected to severe torture by his master, Umayyah ibn Khalaf. To break his spirit, they dragged him across the scorching desert sands and placed heavy rocks on his chest. Yet Bilal kept uttering "Ahad, Ahad" ("One, One"), professing the oneness of God. Eventually, he was freed by Abu Bakr, who paid for his release. Bilal later became the first muezzin (caller to prayer) in Islam, exemplifying how the oppressed could rise to positions of honor within the new community.

4.4.3 Ammar ibn Yasir

Ammar was the son of Sumayyah and Yasir. He witnessed the torture and death of his parents. Ammar himself was forced to utter words against Islam under extreme duress. Deeply distressed, he later turned to Muhammad, who reassured him that God understands the condition of one's heart when torture compels them to speak falsehoods. Ammar's plight demonstrated the harsh realities faced by new Muslims and the compassion Islam offered to believers in distress.

4.5 The Role of the Quran During Persecution

4.5.1 Spiritual Consolation

Revelations during this period offered consolation and encouragement. Some verses emphasized that previous prophets and their followers also faced ridicule and hardship. The Quran reminded believers that God's support remains constant, urging them to remain patient and steadfast. These messages held great emotional power for persecuted Muslims.

4.5.2 Examples from Earlier Prophets

Passages referencing Noah, Abraham, Moses, and Jesus appeared in the revelations. They illustrated how divine messages throughout history encountered resistance from local communities, especially from those clinging to wealth and power. Muslims drew parallels between those prophets' struggles and their own, finding reassurance that righteous perseverance would eventually prevail.

4.5.3 Calls for Patience and Forgiveness

In several places, the Quran advised Muslims against seeking revenge and stressed patience (sabr) and forgiveness. The new community, small and lacking military power, found guidance in these verses to respond with patience rather than violence. The revelations promoted moral fortitude, teaching believers to maintain integrity despite hostile treatment.

4.6 Migration to Abyssinia (First Hijrah)

4.6.1 Reasons for Migration

As persecution intensified, Muhammad permitted some followers to seek refuge in Abyssinia (modern-day Ethiopia), which was ruled by a Christian king, the Negus (Najashi). Abyssinia had a long tradition of religious tolerance, and it seemed like a secure haven for those suffering in Mecca. This event, known as the First Hijrah (migration), took place around the fifth year of Muhammad's prophethood.

4.6.2 Safe Haven Under the Negus

A group of around fifteen Muslims (including men and women) crossed the Red Sea and presented themselves before the Negus. Fearing that this migration might lend credibility to Muhammad's message, the Quraysh sent envoys to demand the refugees' return. However, after hearing the Muslims recite verses from the Quran about Jesus and Mary, the Negus was moved. He refused to hand them over, allowing them to live in Abyssinia peacefully for a time.

4.6.3 Impact on Meccan Perceptions

The migration to Abyssinia signaled that Islam was not just a local issue. The willingness of a foreign Christian ruler to protect Muslim refugees disturbed the Quraysh. They realized the new faith could gain sympathizers beyond the Arabian Peninsula. Still, they doubled down on their opposition back home, determined to isolate Muhammad's community.

4.7 The Boycott and Social Strain

4.7.1 Imposition of a Boycott

In an effort to force Muhammad into submission, the Quraysh enacted a comprehensive boycott against the Hashim and Muttalib clans (whether Muslim or not), who were seen as protective of Muhammad. The boycott was recorded in a document hung in the Ka'bah, declaring that no one should trade, marry, or have social dealings with these clans.

4.7.2 Life in the Ravine

The targeted families moved to a ravine or valley on the outskirts of Mecca, known as Sh'ib Abi Talib. Cut off from supplies, they suffered hunger and hardship. Children cried from lack of food, and some accounts describe how leaves were used to stave off starvation. Yet, the boycott did not break their resolve. Occasional sympathizers from other Quraysh clans smuggled provisions to them, risking punishment.

4.7.3 End of the Boycott

After about two to three years, the boycott collapsed when some fair-minded Quraysh leaders, disturbed by the suffering, campaigned to end it. Legend says that insects had eaten away the document's text except for the phrase mentioning God's name. Regardless of the exact details, the ban was lifted, allowing the families to return to Mecca. The unity shown by the Hashim and Muttalib clans during this ordeal strengthened Muslim morale.

4.8 The Year of Sorrow

4.8.1 Death of Khadijah

Shortly after the boycott ended, Muhammad faced the loss of his beloved wife, Khadijah. She had been his closest confidante, the first to embrace his prophethood, and a constant source of emotional and material support. Her death left a deep void. Muslims consider Khadijah one of the greatest women in Islamic history, respected for her loyalty, generosity, and unwavering faith.

4.8.2 Death of Abu Talib

Not long after Khadijah passed away, Abu Talib also died. As Muhammad's uncle and clan leader, Abu Talib had provided protection that shielded Muhammad from more severe persecution. With Abu Talib gone, the Prophet lost an influential figure who, despite never formally accepting Islam, defended him out of familial loyalty.

4.8.3 Intensification of Hostility

With both Khadijah and Abu Talib gone, the situation in Mecca grew more dangerous. The Prophet's personal grief was compounded by a worsening social and political climate. Historians refer to this period as the "Year of Sorrow." These losses forced Muhammad and the Muslim community to look for alternative ways to continue their mission in an increasingly hostile environment.

4.9 Attempts to Preach Outside Mecca

4.9.1 Journey to Ta'if

After seeing little success in Mecca, Muhammad traveled to Ta'if, a nearby town known for agriculture and wealth, hoping to find supporters or a more receptive audience. However, the leaders of Ta'if rejected his message and, worse, incited local children and thugs to pelt him with stones. Injured and humiliated, Muhammad sought refuge in a vineyard. Despite this harsh rejection, he did not curse his attackers. Instead, he prayed for guidance and mercy.

4.9.2 Minor Support from Strangers

On his way back to Mecca from Ta'if, Muhammad met some jinn (as the Quran narrates) or a small group of strangers who listened to his recitation of the Quran. They acknowledged its truth. This incident showed that while the people of Ta'if spurned his call, others, even from the invisible world of jinn according to Islamic tradition, found guidance in the Quran. Such stories encouraged believers to remain hopeful.

4.9.3 Need for a Broader Support Base

Muhammad realized that the future of Islam in Mecca seemed precarious. With hostility mounting and few prospects in neighboring towns, the Muslims were in search of a larger community that might accept their faith. This quest would eventually lead to the pivotal event of migration to Medina (then called Yathrib), but for now, they remained in Mecca, persevering against difficulties.

4.10 Gradual Growth Despite Hardship

4.10.1 Quiet Conversions

Despite the pressure, new individuals continued to convert. Some were drawn by the moral teachings of the Quran, while others were moved by Muhammad's patience, courage, and evident sincerity. The sincerity of early converts like Bilal and Ammar, who endured torture yet stayed devoted, also inspired onlookers who questioned the depth of their own idol-based beliefs.

4.10.2 Influence of Abu Bakr and Other Leaders

Abu Bakr, a man of kindness and respected standing, used his influence to buy freedom for several slaves who had embraced Islam. His actions spoke volumes about the ethical shift Islam encouraged. Other noteworthy converts included Umar ibn al-Khattab, initially an enemy of Islam, who famously changed his stance after hearing the Quran's verses in his sister's home. Umar's conversion was a significant boost for the Muslim community, as he was known for his strong will and leadership potential.

4.10.3 Stealthy Gatherings for Prayer

With tension running high, Muslims often prayed in secluded areas. When Umar converted, he insisted on praying openly near the Ka'bah, signaling a change in confidence. Though persecution continued, such actions showed that Islam was no longer confined to secret worship. More clan members began to question the harsh tactics used against the Muslims, wondering if they were truly justified.

4.11 Revelation During Adversity

4.11.1 Verses Addressing Persecution

A number of Quranic verses revealed at this time provided guidance on enduring persecution. They spoke of earlier prophets who faced rejection, reassuring Muslims that truth eventually triumphs. For instance, stories of Moses' confrontation with Pharaoh were recounted to illustrate how oppressive rulers succumb to divine justice in the end.

4.11.2 Prohibition of Forced Conversion

Despite facing hostility, Muslims were not permitted to force their beliefs on others. The Quran stated, "There is no compulsion in religion." Even in an environment of significant antagonism, the message remained that hearts must turn to truth willingly. This principle distinguished Islam's approach from that of some other movements that might resort to coercion.

4.11.3 Building Morale and Unity

The revelations also aimed to build solidarity within the Muslim community. Surahs emphasizing the blessings of unity and mutual support encouraged believers to stand together. They were urged to trust God's plan, practice patience, and keep faith in ultimate victory. These themes helped maintain a sense of collective identity and purpose, even as opposition intensified.

4.12 Signs of Transformation in Mecca

4.12.1 Gradual Shift in Public Opinion

Over time, some Meccans who had not accepted Islam softened their stance. They observed the Muslims' conduct: caring for the poor, showing honesty in trade, and refusing to engage in idol worship. The sincerity and consistency of these believers raised questions about whether the Quraysh had been too quick to condemn Muhammad.

4.12.2 The Influence of the Quran's Language

The literary beauty of the Quran continued to captivate many Arabs. Those who prided themselves on poetry found themselves unable to deny the unique power of the verses. Some stealthily listened at night to Muhammad's recitations near his home. These clandestine listeners would return to their clans, discussing the extraordinary nature of this scripture.

4.12.3 Growing Number of Muslims

While still a minority, the Muslim community in Mecca was no longer negligible. The conversions of influential figures like Hamzah (the Prophet's uncle) and Umar ibn al-Khattab provided moral and physical support. Although direct conflict with the Quraysh elite remained dangerous, the new faith was no longer limited to the weakest segments of society.

4.13 The Second Migration to Abyssinia

4.13.1 Larger Group Departs

As Quraysh oppression grew fiercer, another wave of Muslims fled to Abyssinia. This time, a larger group of around a hundred people made the journey. Among them were prominent individuals who would later play roles in Islamic history. Once again, the Negus of Abyssinia provided them asylum.

4.13.2 Diplomatic Maneuvers by the Quraysh

The Quraysh sent representatives to demand the Muslims' extradition. They attempted to frame the Muslims as rebels against Meccan tradition. However, upon listening to the Muslims' statement of faith—highlighting respect for Jesus as a prophet and Mary as a virtuous figure—the Negus recognized common ground with Christian doctrine. He refused to return the refugees, reaffirming their right to live under his protection.

4.13.3 Consequences for Meccan Affairs

These migrations reflected both the severity of persecution and the willingness of some communities to protect the oppressed. The Quraysh grew more frustrated, fearing that Islam's reach extended beyond Mecca's borders. Still, they would not relent in their determination to stifle Muhammad's mission at home.

4.14 Strategic Alliances

4.14.1 Looking North to Yathrib (Medina)

Although not widely known at the time, seeds of the most significant alliance for the Muslims were beginning to sprout in Yathrib (later called Medina). Some people from Yathrib who visited Mecca during the annual pilgrimage heard Muhammad's message. Intrigued, they took it back to their relatives. Given the tribal feuds and social divisions in Yathrib, they hoped a prophet could unify them. This interest would later lead to secret pledges and, eventually, the famous Hijrah to Medina.

4.14.2 Incremental Outreach

While dealing with persecution, Muhammad maintained a vision for peaceful conversion. He met various tribes visiting Mecca, inviting them to Islam. He also sought to build goodwill by offering moral and practical advice based on Quranic teachings. Little by little, the name of the new religion spread beyond the local conflict in Mecca, reaching distant tribes through word of mouth.

4.14.3 The Importance of Tribal Dynamics

Tribal alliances were key to survival in Arabia. A single clan could offer collective defense, while alliances with multiple tribes enhanced security. For Islam to gain a stable base, it needed the protection of a community willing to accept Muhammad's message wholeheartedly. The experiences in Mecca—marked by hostility—confirmed that a different environment might be necessary for the faith to flourish.

4.15 Lessons from the Meccan Period

4.15.1 Perseverance in the Face of Adversity

The hardships Muslims endured during the Meccan period taught them resilience. They learned that faith cannot be built on convenience; it requires sacrifice and sincerity. This lesson would prove invaluable in later conflicts and challenges.

4.15.2 Moral Conduct as a Form of Dawah (Invitation)

The best argument for Islam in these early years was often the believers' upright conduct. Their honesty, patience, and generosity attracted curious onlookers. Even enemies of Islam sometimes admitted they could not fault the ethical behavior of Muhammad and his followers.

4.15.3 The Role of Revelation in Community Formation

The Quranic revelations were not abstract theology. They addressed real struggles in real time, guiding believers on how to handle persecution, loss, and hope. The revelations bound the community together, fostering a sense of shared destiny and divine support.

Chapter Five: Migration to Medina and the Formation of a Community

5.1 Introduction

By the early 620s CE, the Muslim community in Mecca had grown steadily but faced severe opposition. The death of key supporters like Khadijah and Abu Talib made the Prophet Muhammad and his followers more vulnerable to harassment from Meccan leaders. Despite this difficulty, a new opportunity arose in Yathrib (later known as Medina), a city some 300 kilometers north of Mecca. Certain residents of Yathrib showed interest in Muhammad's message, hoping it might help resolve long-standing tribal conflicts in their city.

In this chapter, we will examine the circumstances that led to the Hijrah (migration) from Mecca to Medina, one of the most significant turning points in Islamic history. We will explore the pledges made by the people of Yathrib, the cautious planning that enabled the Muslims to leave Mecca safely, and the warm reception they received upon arrival. We will then describe the Prophet's steps to unify his followers and establish a solid, faith-based community in Medina. This includes the construction of the Prophet's Mosque, the formation of a brotherhood between the emigrants (Muhajirun) and the helpers (Ansar), and the creation of the Constitution of Medina. These events laid the groundwork for a new social and political order guided by the principles found in the Quranic revelations.

5.2 Background: Yathrib's Internal Conflicts

5.2.1 The Aws and Khazraj Tribes

Before the arrival of Islam, Yathrib was home to two major Arab tribes, the Aws and the Khazraj. For years, these tribes had engaged in bitter feuds and intermittent warfare. Smaller sub-tribes and allied Jewish communities also inhabited the region. Though Yathrib was blessed with agriculture—particularly date palms and fertile oases—its social stability was fragile.

The Aws and Khazraj were often locked in power struggles, each seeking allies to gain an advantage over the other. Civil wars brought destruction, leading many people to long for a mediator who could bring genuine peace. Rumors of a prophet in Mecca who spoke of unity, fairness, and devotion to one God began to circulate. Some in Yathrib viewed this prophet as a potential solution to their internal chaos.

5.2.2 Early Contacts with Muhammad

During the annual pilgrimage season in Mecca, individuals from Yathrib would travel to the Ka'bah for traditional rites (even though these predated the Islamic Hajj). On one such visit, a small group from the Khazraj encountered Muhammad. Impressed by his call for monotheism and moral reform, they invited him to speak more about his faith. They saw in his teachings a path toward reconciliation in their troubled city.

Over time, more people from Yathrib met with Muhammad in Mecca, learning about the Quran's emphasis on worshiping one God, helping the needy, and abandoning idolatry. This laid the groundwork for formal pledges that would ultimately lead to the Muslims' migration.

5.3 The Pledges of Aqaba

5.3.1 The First Pledge

A key milestone in forging a bond between Muhammad and the people of Yathrib was the First Pledge of Aqaba (around 621 CE). At a spot known as Aqaba near Mina (outside Mecca), a small group of Yathrib residents covertly met the Prophet at night to affirm their belief in one God and their acceptance of Muhammad as His messenger. They promised to refrain from idol worship, theft, infanticide, and any major sins. However, this first pledge did not yet include any direct commitment to defend Muhammad physically.

Muhammad sent a knowledgeable companion, Mus'ab ibn Umair, back to Yathrib with them to teach the Quran and the basics of Islam. Mus'ab's presence in Yathrib helped the new converts learn their faith more deeply, and he engaged in discussions with various tribal leaders to calm tensions and share Islamic beliefs.

5.3.2 The Second Pledge

A year later (around 622 CE), a larger group from Yathrib returned to Mecca for pilgrimage. In secret, they met again with Muhammad at Aqaba and made a more binding agreement, known as the Second Pledge of Aqaba. This time, they pledged not only to uphold Islamic teachings but also to defend the Prophet if he came to Yathrib. They agreed to treat him as one of their own, defending him even against external threats.

This second pledge was significant because it signaled that the Prophet and his followers could find a secure base in Yathrib. The new faith would no longer be confined to a small persecuted group in Mecca. By agreeing to protect him, the people of Yathrib effectively granted Muhammad leadership among them. This transformation was vital, as the Muslims in Mecca desperately needed a place where they could practice their faith openly without fear of violence.

5.4 Plans for Migration and Meccan Opposition

5.4.1 The Decision to Migrate

After the Second Pledge of Aqaba, Muhammad encouraged his followers in Mecca to migrate to Yathrib in small groups. Many left quietly to avoid drawing attention. The Quraysh suspected something was afoot. They recognized that if Muhammad found a supportive community elsewhere, their efforts to stifle Islam might fail. But for the moment, Meccan leaders did not fully grasp the scale of the migration.

5.4.2 The Quraysh's Gathering

When it became clear that Muslims were leaving in increasing numbers, the Quraysh convened a council known as Dar al-Nadwah. Various proposals arose to deal with Muhammad decisively. Some suggested imprisoning him, while others advocated exile. Finally, a more drastic plan emerged: each clan would contribute one warrior, and they would collectively assassinate Muhammad. This way, responsibility for his death would be spread among many clans, discouraging any single clan from seeking blood vengeance.

5.4.3 Divine Guidance and the Escape Plan

According to Islamic tradition, God informed Muhammad of the assassination plot. He was directed to leave Mecca under the cover of night. Muhammad asked his close friend Abu Bakr to accompany him. Ali, Muhammad's young cousin, volunteered to sleep in the Prophet's bed to create the illusion he was still at home, thus buying time for the escape. When the assassins peered into the house, they saw a sleeping figure and assumed their target was still there. Meanwhile, Muhammad and Abu Bakr slipped away.

5.5 The Hijrah: Journey to Yathrib

5.5.1 Departure and the Cave of Thawr

Muhammad and Abu Bakr initially traveled south of Mecca—a direction opposite to Yathrib—to confuse their pursuers. They hid in the Cave of Thawr for several days, with Abu Bakr's family covertly bringing them food and intelligence on Quraysh movements. At one point, the pursuers nearly discovered the cave. However, they were deterred by what they perceived as natural signs, such as a spiderweb at the cave's entrance and a nesting bird, suggesting that nobody had entered recently.

5.5.2 The Desert Trek

After the danger subsided, Muhammad and Abu Bakr hired a skilled guide to lead them through lesser-known routes toward Yathrib. The journey was arduous, spanning days under the intense Arabian sun. Despite the physical hardship, traditions describe the Prophet and Abu Bakr exchanging encouraging words, buoyed by faith that God was protecting them. Their slow yet determined progress through the desert forged an enduring bond.

5.5.3 Arriving at Quba

On the outskirts of Yathrib, in an area known as Quba, Muhammad and his companion were greeted by local Muslims who had eagerly awaited his arrival. He stayed there briefly, helping to found what is considered the first mosque in Islam, known today as the Quba Mosque. This place of worship represented the new beginning for a community free from Meccan persecution.

5.6 Reception in Yathrib and the City's Renaming

5.6.1 Entrance into the City

When news spread that Muhammad had reached Quba safely, many residents of Yathrib gathered along the roads to welcome him. Children sang songs of praise, marking his safe arrival. Different clans vied to host the Prophet, each hoping to honor him. According to tradition, Muhammad let his camel roam freely, allowing it to stop where it chose. It finally knelt on a plot of land owned by two orphan brothers near the homes of the Banu Najjar clan (relatives of the Prophet's grandfather on his mother's side). Muhammad purchased this plot to build a mosque and a modest dwelling.

5.6.2 "Medinat an-Nabi"

Over time, Yathrib became known as "Medinat an-Nabi" (the City of the Prophet), often shortened to Medina. In the years that followed, it would serve as the political and spiritual center of the nascent Islamic community. This migration event, or Hijrah, marked such a turning point in Islamic history that the Muslim calendar begins with this year, typically noted as 622 CE in the Gregorian calendar.

5.6.3 A Diverse Community

Medina was home not only to the Aws and Khazraj tribes but also to several Jewish tribes (such as Banu Qaynuqa, Banu Nadir, and Banu Qurayzah). With the arrival of the Meccan Muslims (the Muhajirun), the population became more diverse. Integrating these different groups into a single, cohesive society would require wisdom, compromise, and clear guidelines.

5.7 Establishment of the Prophet's Mosque

5.7.1 Building a Physical and Spiritual Center

One of Muhammad's first actions was to build a central mosque on the land where his camel had stopped. He participated alongside his companions in laying bricks and carrying materials, illustrating the principle that leaders should work alongside their followers. This mosque, known in Arabic as "Masjid an-Nabawi," was initially a simple structure with walls made of sun-dried bricks, a roof of palm leaves, and pillars of palm trunks.

Despite its simplicity, the mosque became the heartbeat of Medina's Islamic life. It served as a place for prayer, public gatherings, legal discussions, and social welfare activities. The Prophet would address the community from there, receive delegations, and offer guidance rooted in the ongoing Quranic revelations.

5.7.2 Adjacent Rooms for the Prophet's Family

Attached to the mosque, small living quarters were constructed for the Prophet and his family. These quarters were modest, reflecting the overall emphasis on simplicity and humility. Over time, more structures would be added, but the primary intent was to keep the mosque accessible to all, reinforcing the sense that worship and daily life were interconnected in the new Muslim community.

5.7.3 A Symbol of Unity

The communal effort involved in building the mosque and the direct involvement of Muhammad set an example of shared responsibility. As new revelations guided them, the Muslims in Medina began to see the mosque not just as a place of ritual but as the physical symbol of the unity they shared under Islam. For the emigrants (Muhajirun) from Mecca, the mosque offered a sense of belonging in a new city. For the helpers (Ansar) of Medina, it was a chance to bond with their new brothers in faith.

5.8 Brotherhood Between Muhajirun and Ansar

5.8.1 Pairing Individuals from Mecca and Medina

Another significant step in forming a cohesive society was the Prophet's institution of brotherhood (Mu'akhah) between specific Muhajirun (Meccan emigrants) and specific Ansar (local helpers). In this arrangement, each Ansari family would pair with an emigrant family, sharing resources, lodging, and support. For many Meccan Muslims who left behind property and businesses, this arrangement offered immediate relief from destitution.

5.8.2 Economic and Emotional Support

This brotherhood was more than a token gesture. It involved mutual inheritance rights in the earliest stage, which was unusual in a tribal context where inheritance typically stayed within blood relations. Though later verses of the Quran would clarify inheritance laws, this initial measure underscored the seriousness of the bond. It created a familial atmosphere between people of different tribes and backgrounds, reducing the sense of alienation among the newcomers.

5.8.3 Spirit of Cooperation

The spirit of cooperation that emerged set Medina apart from other regions. Instead of old tribal rivalries, relationships were based on shared faith and mutual support. Wealthy members of the Ansar often offered farmland or assistance in setting up new businesses for the emigrants. This arrangement represented a practical application of Islamic values like charity, brotherhood, and compassion.

5.9 The Constitution of Medina

5.9.1 A Social and Political Framework

Soon after settling in Medina, Muhammad oversaw the drafting of a social contract often referred to as the "Constitution of Medina." This document aimed to regulate relationships among the diverse groups in Medina: the Muhajirun, the Ansar, and the Jewish tribes. It addressed issues like collective defense, resolving disputes, religious freedom, and mutual respect.

5.9.2 Key Principles

1. **Unity as One Community**: The document declared all signatories as forming a single community (Ummah), despite religious differences. Muslims and Jews would remain distinct in their faiths but form a pact of mutual defense and cooperation.
2. **Protection of Life and Property**: It specified that all parties must safeguard one another's security. Blood feuds, once common in Arabia, were discouraged.
3. **Respect for Religious Practices**: Jewish tribes could maintain their religious laws and customs. Similarly, the Muslims would follow the Quranic teachings without interference.
4. **Joint Defense**: In case of attack from an external enemy, all groups would defend Medina. Costs of defense would be shared proportionally.
5. **Right to Justice**: Disputes would be referred to Muhammad as an arbiter. The Constitution established a process for conflict resolution, ensuring fairness for each party.

5.9.3 Significance of the Charter

The Constitution of Medina is considered groundbreaking for its time. It shifted loyalty from purely tribal lines toward a broader communal identity. While it did not erase tribal affiliations entirely, it placed overarching emphasis on collective welfare and justice. This social contract helped stabilize Medina, reducing factional tension and setting the stage for the city to become a stable base for Islamic expansion in the following years.

5.10 Early Challenges in Medina

5.10.1 Economic Hardships

Though the bonds of brotherhood provided some relief, the emigrants had left behind wealth and property in Mecca. In Medina, agriculture dominated the economy, and not all emigrants had the skills or resources to farm immediately. Many needed time to adjust. The local community had to balance providing for their own families and aiding the newcomers. Quranic verses would later encourage communal charity (zakat) and voluntary giving (sadaqah) as ways to support those in need.

5.10.2 Relations with Jewish Tribes

The Jewish tribes in Medina had their own established traditions, scriptures, and social structures. While some individuals were friendly or even interested in Muhammad's teachings, others remained wary of changes. The Constitution of Medina provided a framework for coexistence, but underlying tensions occasionally surfaced, often fueled by political and economic rivalries.

5.10.3 Threats from Mecca

The Quraysh in Mecca were alarmed by Muhammad's successful integration into Medina. They recognized that the Prophet now had a supportive base and might challenge their trade routes. Sporadic skirmishes and provocations began, setting the stage for future armed conflicts. In addition, Meccan leaders pressured other tribes not to aid the Muslims, using alliances and trade embargoes to isolate Medina.

5.11 Role of the Quran in Community Building

5.11.1 Ongoing Revelations

In Medina, Muhammad continued to receive revelations that addressed the community's evolving needs. While the Meccan surahs primarily focused on matters of faith and the afterlife, Medinan surahs included more legal and social directives. Examples include guidelines on marriage, dietary rules, inheritance, and community cohesion.

5.11.2 Moral and Legal Instructions

The revelations encouraged Muslims to uphold justice, extend mercy to the poor, and form strong family ties. New regulations such as the prohibition of interest (riba) aimed to prevent economic exploitation. The Quran also urged believers to maintain strong bonds with their relatives and look after orphans. These instructions shaped Medina's social fabric, gradually moving it away from tribal vendettas and exploitative practices.

5.11.3 Spiritual Life Centered Around the Mosque

With the Prophet's Mosque as the community's heart, daily prayer became an integral part of life. Gathering multiple times a day reinforced unity and consistency of purpose. Quranic recitation at these prayers reminded Muslims of their shared faith and identity, keeping them focused on ethical and spiritual goals despite external challenges.

5.12 Building Alliances Beyond Medina

5.12.1 Diplomatic Efforts

Although Medina was now a stable base, it was vulnerable to attacks from hostile tribes. Muhammad initiated diplomatic engagements with neighboring Bedouin and settled communities, aiming to secure peace pacts or neutrality agreements. Letters and envoys introduced Islam's message, but equally important, they established the possibility of non-aggression.

5.12.2 The Strategic Importance of Trade Routes

Mecca had dominated trade in the Hijaz region for generations, benefiting from caravans passing through. With the Muslims now in Medina, the strategic trade routes could be redirected or threatened. The Prophet sought to establish safe passages for trading caravans associated with the Muslim community, thereby challenging Meccan dominance. These economic shifts fueled Meccan hostility even further.

5.12.3 Early Skirmishes

Some minor encounters took place between Muslim scouting parties and Quraysh caravans. These were not large-scale conflicts, but they tested the readiness of the Muslim community to defend itself. The revelations in this period allowed defensive measures if Muslims were attacked, emphasizing that fighting was permitted only when oppression and aggression were clear.

5.13 Significance of the Hijrah

5.13.1 A New Phase for Islam

The migration to Medina fundamentally changed the status of the Muslims. In Mecca, they were a persecuted minority. In Medina, they became an organized community with a sense of belonging and growing political influence. This shift also changed the nature of the revelations, which now included governance, law, and communal obligations.

5.13.2 Establishing a Model Society

Over time, Medina came to symbolize what a faith-based community could achieve. By bridging gaps between tribes, promoting unity, and implementing social justice, the Medinan community served as a living example of Quranic principles. Although not without problems, it showcased the possibility of ethical governance in a region long plagued by tribal conflict.

5.13.3 The Start of the Islamic Calendar

In later Islamic history, the caliph Umar ibn al-Khattab officially adopted the Hijrah year as the starting point of the Muslim calendar. This decision reflected the profound importance of the migration. It was not the date of the first revelation, nor the date of the Prophet's birth, but rather the formation of an Islamic society that was chosen as the epoch for Muslim reckoning of time.

5.14 Lessons from the Medinan Transition

5.14.1 Perseverance Yields New Opportunities

The hardships endured in Mecca prepared the Muslims for greater challenges. Their steadfast faith, tested by persecution, served them well in Medina. The open environment enabled the message of Islam to develop and expand more effectively.

5.14.2 Importance of Leadership and Vision

Muhammad's leadership was crucial for uniting diverse groups in Medina. He balanced the spiritual dimensions of his role with practical governance, showing that religion and day-to-day affairs could be integrated harmoniously. This approach laid a foundation for future Islamic governance models.

5.14.3 Gradual Community Building

The progress in Medina was not instantaneous. It evolved through careful measures like the Constitution of Medina, the pairing of Muhajirun and Ansar, and the shared construction of the mosque. Each step promoted cooperation and mutual respect, reflecting Quranic calls for unity and justice.

Chapter Six: The Quranic Revelations in Medina

6.1 Introduction

With the Muslim community now established in Medina, the nature of the Quranic revelations began to shift. During the Meccan period, verses primarily emphasized core beliefs about the oneness of God, the afterlife, and moral responsibility. In Medina, the context changed significantly. Muslims were no longer a small, persecuted group but a community in need of detailed guidance on social, legal, and political matters.

In this chapter, we will explore how the Quranic revelations in Medina differed from those in Mecca. We will discuss the introduction of new forms of worship, the development of laws governing society, and the Quran's approach to interfaith relations—especially concerning Jewish and Christian communities. We will also look at how these revelations were preserved, focusing on the role of scribes, memorization, and practical application in daily life.

6.2 Differences Between Meccan and Medinan Revelations

6.2.1 Shifts in Tone and Subject Matter

The Meccan surahs largely focused on establishing faith in one God, warning of the Day of Judgment, and offering comfort to believers enduring persecution.

After the Hijrah, the Medinan surahs took on a more legislative and communal tone. They addressed issues like marriage, inheritance, criminal justice, dietary laws, and diplomatic relations—topics essential for running a functioning society.

6.2.2 Length and Structure

Medinan surahs tend to be longer than many Meccan chapters. They contain more detailed instructions and often address current events. These verses would sometimes be revealed in response to specific questions or incidents. This situational aspect made the revelations directly relevant to the believers' everyday lives, ensuring that divine guidance aligned with immediate communal needs.

6.2.3 Emphasis on Unity and Social Cohesion

While Meccan verses did highlight moral virtues, Medinan revelations emphasized collective responsibility. The Muslim community had to deal with internal disputes, external threats, and alliances with non-Muslim groups. The Quran continued to stress piety and righteousness but linked these virtues to the practical realities of maintaining justice in a diverse society.

6.3 Establishing Key Acts of Worship

6.3.1 Five Daily Prayers (Salah)

Although prayer was established in Mecca, the structure of five daily prayers became more clearly defined in Medina. Believers congregated in the Prophet's Mosque at dawn, noon, mid-afternoon, sunset, and night. The community aspect of prayer reinforced social ties. Over time, the call to prayer (Adhan) was introduced, famously called by Bilal ibn Rabah. This call replaced earlier methods of summoning people to pray and became a distinctive feature of Islamic life.

6.3.2 Fasting in Ramadan

The command to fast during the month of Ramadan was instituted in Medina (Quran 2:183-187). Fasting became a community-wide act of devotion, self-discipline, and empathy for the less fortunate. The revelations about fasting outlined the basic rules: abstaining from food and drink from dawn until sunset, followed by a meal after sunset (Iftar). Exemptions were given to the sick, travelers, and others unable to fast, reflecting the Quran's principle of compassion.

6.3.3 Zakat (Mandatory Charity)

While charity was encouraged in Mecca, the formal institution of Zakat, or mandatory almsgiving, took shape in Medina. Specific guidelines were revealed on how much wealth to give and to whom. This included orphans, the poor, travelers in need, and others in vulnerable positions. Zakat helped redistribute wealth in a way that reduced poverty and promoted social cohesion.

6.3.4 Hajj and Umrah Guidelines

Though pilgrimage to the Ka'bah was a pre-Islamic practice, the Quranic guidelines for Hajj and Umrah (the lesser pilgrimage) were clarified during the Medinan period. However, because Mecca was still under Quraysh control until its eventual peaceful conquest (years later), Muslims in Medina had limited access to perform these rites freely at that time. Nevertheless, the revelations laid the groundwork for how Muslims should conduct the pilgrimage once they could safely return to Mecca.

6.4 The Change of Qiblah

6.4.1 Praying Toward Jerusalem

In the early Medinan period, Muslims initially prayed facing Jerusalem, aligning themselves with the Qiblah used by Jews living in Medina. This practice highlighted the connection between Islam and previous Abrahamic faiths, demonstrating respect for the shared heritage of monotheism.

6.4.2 Revelation to Face the Ka'bah

After some months in Medina, a significant revelation (Quran 2:142-150) directed Muslims to turn their faces toward the Ka'bah in Mecca during prayer. The Prophet Muhammad received this instruction while leading a congregational prayer. Obedient to the command, he changed direction in mid-prayer. This event is referred to as the "Tahwil al-Qiblah" (the change of the prayer direction).

6.4.3 Significance of the Shift

The Qiblah change had several implications:

1. **Distinct Identity**: It affirmed that Islam, while acknowledging the line of earlier prophets, had its own unique direction of worship.
2. **Connection to Abraham**: The Ka'bah was believed to have been built by Abraham (Ibrahim) and his son Ishmael (Isma'il). Praying toward this sanctuary linked the Muslim community to Abraham's pure monotheism.
3. **Test of Obedience**: The Quran described this event as a trial of faith, seeing who would accept the new direction without hesitation and who might struggle with the change.

6.5 Revelation on Warfare and Defense

6.5.1 Permission to Fight Oppression

Unlike in Mecca, where Muslims were instructed to endure persecution, the Medinan verses allowed them to defend themselves militarily. Quran 22:39-40 declares that permission is granted to those who are fought against because they have been wronged. These verses highlighted the justice-based rationale: Muslims should fight only when oppressed or expelled from their homes.

6.5.2 Ethics of Warfare

The Quranic instructions emphasized restraint. Civilians and non-combatants (such as women, children, and the elderly) were not to be harmed. Destroying crops, trees, or other resources unnecessarily was discouraged. If the enemy ceased hostilities, Muslims were instructed to stop fighting. This balanced approach aimed to prevent aggression while allowing the community to survive in a hostile environment.

6.5.3 Early Conflicts: Badr, Uhud, and Beyond

Shortly after settling in Medina, the Muslims found themselves in confrontation with the Quraysh. The Battle of Badr (624 CE) was the first major encounter, where a smaller Muslim force unexpectedly triumphed against a larger Meccan army. Quranic verses related to Badr reassured believers that victory was a sign of divine support. However, subsequent battles like Uhud showed that Muslims were not guaranteed victory if they disobeyed the Prophet's instructions or became overconfident. The revelations often provided immediate commentary on these events, guiding the community's moral and strategic choices.

6.6 Social and Family Laws

6.6.1 Marriage and Family Structure

Medinan revelations outlined regulations for marriage, divorce, and family responsibilities. For instance, multiple verses in Surah An-Nisa (Chapter 4) explained conditions under which polygamy was permissible, emphasizing justice among spouses. The Quran also encouraged kindness and proper treatment of wives, widows, and orphans. By providing these laws, the community could address family disputes with clear guidance.

6.6.2 Inheritance Laws

Another significant area of legislation was inheritance. Pre-Islamic Arabia did not always give women or orphaned children fair shares of family property. The Quran introduced detailed inheritance rules (notably in Surah An-Nisa) to ensure that each relative—male or female—received an assigned share. This helped stabilize families by preventing arbitrary decisions and injustice.

6.6.3 Prohibitions on Alcohol and Gambling

In Mecca, the Quran had hinted at the negative effects of intoxicants and gambling, but outright prohibition came later in Medina. Step by step, verses revealed that alcohol and gambling sowed discord and harm, culminating in a final ban (Quran 5:90-91). This gradual approach allowed people to adjust to the new norms, reflecting a broader Quranic method of phased legislation.

6.7 Relations with the People of the Book

6.7.1 Shared Roots of Faith

In Medina, Muslims lived alongside Jewish tribes and occasionally interacted with Christians in diplomatic contexts. The Quran acknowledged shared reverence for prophets like Moses and Jesus, calling Jews and Christians "People of the Book." Medinan verses encouraged dialogue, urging them to unite around the worship of one God and moral teachings rooted in their scriptures.

6.7.2 Areas of Tension

While the Constitution of Medina initially established a framework for peaceful coexistence with Jewish tribes, political and economic disputes sometimes caused strains. Some Jewish tribes supported Meccan forces in conflicts against the Muslims, leading to tensions that eventually escalated. The Quran addressed these issues by distinguishing between those who honored agreements and those who betrayed them, rather than condemning an entire community indiscriminately.

6.7.3 Interfaith Conduct

The Medinan revelations provided guidelines on interfaith marriage (allowing Muslim men to marry chaste women from the People of the Book) and dietary rules. Believers were permitted to eat meat slaughtered by Jews and Christians, reflecting a degree of shared dietary norms. These instructions promoted a level of social interaction and respect, though doctrinal differences remained.

6.8 Preservation of the Quran in Medina

6.8.1 Role of the Scribes

With more verses coming, the Prophet had designated scribes to write down revelations. Notable among them was Zayd ibn Thabit, who was from Medina. Zayd learned to read and write at a young age, making him valuable to the Prophet. He and other scribes would record verses on available materials such as parchment, leather, or palm stalks. Whenever a new verse was revealed, Muhammad would call a scribe, recite the verse, and instruct him on which surah (chapter) and position it belonged to, thus maintaining an order for the revelations.

6.8.2 Memorization by the Companions

Oral transmission remained crucial. Many companions memorized large portions, if not the entirety, of the Quran. Recitation in daily prayers and communal gatherings reinforced memory and accuracy. The Prophet also led a yearly review (in Ramadan) with the Angel Gabriel, according to tradition, to confirm the correct arrangement of the revealed text up to that point.

6.8.3 Circulation Among Muslims

As the Muslim community expanded, written fragments and memorized recitations spread beyond Medina to other regions. Skilled reciters, known for their exceptional memory, traveled to teach newly converted tribes. This network of teachers and learners fostered a culture of care in preserving the Quranic text, minimizing the risk of error or alteration.

6.9 Implementation and Practical Applications

6.9.1 Life in the Prophet's Mosque

The Prophet's Mosque served as the central place for Quranic instruction. Questions on legal matters, ethics, and worship were answered here in light of revealed verses. Public recitations ensured everyone could learn new revelations as they were revealed. This setting turned religious learning into a communal, transparent process.

6.9.2 Community Enforcement

When a revelation established a new rule—like the prohibition of alcohol—believers enforced it collectively. Accounts describe that once the final ban on intoxicants was revealed, Muslims poured out remaining stocks of wine into the streets of Medina. The transformation was immediate and community-wide, showing how deeply the revelations influenced daily habits.

6.9.3 Addressing Disputes

People in Medina often brought their disputes—over property, trade, marriage, and other matters—to Muhammad. He would base judgments on Quranic principles. Such rulings guided the community to seek justice and harmony, limiting the old tribal practice of personal revenge. This helped forge a shared legal framework that transcended clan loyalties.

6.10 Challenges from Hypocrisy and Internal Dissent

6.10.1 Emergence of the "Hypocrites"

With Islam's rising influence in Medina, some individuals joined the Muslim community outwardly but did not truly believe in the Prophet's message. These people, known in the Quran as "Munafiqun" (hypocrites), posed internal challenges. They would sometimes spread rumors, question decisions, or sow discord, hoping to undermine Muslim unity.

6.10.2 Quranic Verses Addressing Hypocrisy

Medinan revelations confronted this issue, warning believers to be cautious but also not to judge each other's faith hastily. The Quran pointed out signs of hypocrisy, such as reluctance to participate in communal obligations, secret alliances with enemies, and public statements contradicting private intentions. These verses taught believers to remain vigilant, trust sincere actions, and leave ultimate judgment to God.

6.10.3 Strategies for Community Solidarity

Despite these internal challenges, the Prophet worked to maintain harmony through constant engagement. He encouraged honesty, participation in prayers, and involvement in community welfare as indicators of genuine faith. This approach minimized the impact of hypocrites, though some disruptions occurred during times of crisis or war.

6.11 The Growth of the Muslim Community

6.11.1 Spread of Islam Across Arabia

As more tribes heard about Medina's stability and the Prophet's leadership, delegations arrived to learn about Islam. Some tribes embraced the faith voluntarily; others formed non-aggression pacts. The reputation of the Medinan community as just, organized, and spiritually grounded enhanced its appeal. The Quran played a key role, offering moral and legal guidelines that resonated with many, especially those tired of constant tribal warfare.

6.11.2 Role of Da'wah (Invitation to Islam)

Muhammad sent letters to rulers in regions like Egypt, Persia, and Byzantine territories, inviting them to consider Islam. While immediate large-scale conversions did not occur, these initiatives broadened awareness of the new religion. Meanwhile, smaller tribes and settlements in Arabia increasingly aligned with Medina, contributing to a growing sense of unity under the Prophet's leadership.

6.11.3 The Community's Administrative Evolution

Though not a formal "state" as we think of modern governments, the Medinan community functioned with a growing administrative capacity. The Quran's guidance on contracts, record-keeping (for loans, etc.), and community responsibilities helped shape a system of governance rooted in ethical principles. The Prophet appointed representatives to oversee regions, collect charity, and address local disputes.

6.12 Major Events Influencing Revelation

6.12.1 The Treaty of Hudaybiyyah

In 628 CE, the Muslims attempted a peaceful pilgrimage to Mecca. Stopped by the Quraysh at Hudaybiyyah, they negotiated a truce. The Treaty of Hudaybiyyah gave Muslims a period of peace with Mecca, albeit under conditions that initially seemed unfavorable. Quranic verses reassured believers that this treaty was a "clear victory," suggesting that peace would allow Islam to spread without the constant strain of warfare. Indeed, many tribes soon embraced Islam, leading to a growth in Muslim numbers.

6.12.2 The Conquest of Mecca

By 630 CE, the Quraysh violated the treaty's terms. The Prophet marched on Mecca with a large Muslim force. Meccan leaders, seeing little chance of victory, surrendered peacefully. The Prophet entered the city without major bloodshed and forgave most of his former enemies. The Ka'bah was cleansed of idols, aligning the sanctuary once again with its monotheistic origins. Revelations from this period emphasized gratitude to God, unity among believers, and the abolishing of idolatry in Islam's holiest site.

6.12.3 Farewell Pilgrimage and Final Sermon

In 632 CE, the Prophet performed what is called the Farewell Pilgrimage, where he delivered a sermon emphasizing equality, the sanctity of life and property, and proper treatment of women. Quranic revelations around this time pointed to the completion of God's favor on humanity through Islam. Shortly afterward, the Prophet fell ill and passed away. Many of the final verses addressed matters of piety and the importance of remaining steadfast in faith even after the Prophet's death.

6.13 Summarizing the Medinan Revelation Themes

6.13.1 Legislative Guidance

The Medinan surahs collectively provided the laws necessary to establish a functional and ethical society: family law, economic regulations, inheritance, dietary guidelines, and more. These verses shaped the communal norms for generations to come, serving as a reference for Muslim governance and daily life.

6.13.2 Consolidation of the Community

Under the Prophet's guidance, supported by Quranic instructions, Medina became a cohesive community that integrated faith, culture, and governance. The brotherhood between Muhajirun and Ansar, the Constitution of Medina, and repeated injunctions for cooperation and charity helped create unity in a region once torn by tribal feuds.

6.13.3 Principles of Justice and Diplomacy

The Quran in Medina reinforced justice not only within the Muslim community but also in dealings with other groups. The instructions against betrayal of treaties, the moral codes for warfare, and the respect for other monotheistic faiths positioned Islam as both a religious and political force in Arabia. Diplomacy and conflict resolution were guided by ethical and spiritual values rather than raw tribal power.

Chapter Seven: Compilation Efforts During the Prophet's Lifetime

7.1 Introduction

By the time the Muslim community had established itself in Medina, the Quran had been revealed over a span of more than a decade. The revelations would continue until the final days of Prophet Muhammad's life. During this extensive period, the message arrived in portions, responding to various questions, circumstances, and challenges faced by the community. As the community grew in size and influence, so did the importance of preserving these divine words accurately.

The Prophet took deliberate steps to ensure that the Quran would not be lost or altered. He employed multiple methods: encouraging memorization among his followers, assigning trusted scribes to record verses, and regularly reviewing the revealed passages. In this chapter, we explore the processes that preserved the Quran during the Prophet's lifetime. We will examine the roles of scribes, the community's commitment to memorization, the organization of surahs, and the Prophet's final review with the Angel Jibril (Gabriel). These efforts laid the foundation for a text that would remain consistent long after his death.

7.2 The Nature of Revelation and Gradual Descent

7.2.1 Reasons for Gradual Revelation

The Quran was not revealed in one single moment. Instead, it came down over approximately twenty-three years—thirteen in Mecca and ten in Medina. This gradual process allowed the Muslim community to absorb new laws and concepts incrementally. It also permitted immediate guidance in response to specific events, whether military conflicts, social disputes, or personal questions.

This step-by-step revelation was particularly important in shaping legal and moral practices within the emerging society. For instance, certain prohibitions like alcohol or usury were introduced in stages, giving people time to adapt. The approach reflected a divine wisdom: humans often need a period of transition to change ingrained behaviors. By distributing the revelation over many years, God ensured that believers could integrate each command into daily life without overwhelming disruption.

7.2.2 Verses Arranged in Surahs

Though revealed in small segments, the Quran was ultimately divided into surahs (chapters). However, the order of revelation did not necessarily match the final chapter arrangement. A verse revealed toward the end of the Prophet's life could appear in a surah that started with verses revealed earlier, and vice versa. Whenever a new verse or group of verses came down, the Prophet would instruct the scribes exactly where to place them within the existing structure.

This method created a cohesive yet non-chronological arrangement. Each surah blended verses revealed in both Mecca and Medina. This unique layout emphasized themes and lessons that transcended timeline. Many surahs include reminders of God's oneness, directives on ethical behavior, and references to past prophets' experiences—all interwoven in a way that best served the believers' spiritual needs.

7.2.3 Reviewing and Reciting Among Companions

The Prophet was known to recite newly revealed verses in communal prayers, private study sessions, and gatherings at the mosque. He also instructed specific companions to memorize and teach others. These oral recitations allowed the community to verify the text collectively, increasing the likelihood of accurate transmission. If any mistake arose in a companion's recitation, others who had memorized the verse could correct it on the spot.

Furthermore, the Prophet himself would recite passages repeatedly, particularly during Ramadan, when he engaged in a thorough review with the Angel Jibril. This annual review not only cemented the final arrangement in his mind but also assured the community that the text was being preserved with divine oversight.

7.3 The Role of Scribes

7.3.1 Appointing Trusted Individuals

Prophet Muhammad appointed a number of companions as scribes. Among them, Zayd ibn Thabit is the most well-known. Others included Ubayy ibn Ka'b, Mu'awiyah ibn Abi Sufyan, Abdullah ibn Mas'ud, and Ali ibn Abi Talib, though some were more active as scribes than others. These individuals were chosen for their reliability, literacy, and devotion to the faith.

Many Arabs of that era were skilled in poetry and oral traditions, but formal literacy was less common. Finding a companion who could write legibly on parchment or other materials was therefore significant. Their work had to be meticulous, as any errors in transcription could have lasting consequences. Thus, scribes often wrote while the Prophet dictated or after hearing him recite several times, ensuring accuracy.

7.3.2 Materials Used for Writing

The writing materials of the time were rudimentary and varied. Scribes wrote verses on parchment (processed animal skins), papyrus, thinly treated leather, flat stones, palm tree stalks, and even bones like the shoulder blades of camels. Quality parchment was prized, but scarce. This diversity of writing materials meant that no single, bound volume of the Quran existed during the Prophet's lifetime. Instead, fragments, scrolls, and pieces were stored by different companions.

Such decentralized record-keeping had advantages and disadvantages. On the positive side, distributing written portions among many individuals provided a safeguard against any single source being lost or damaged. On the negative side, collecting everything after the Prophet's passing required careful cross-referencing of these fragments.

7.3.3 Immediate Corrections and Authoritative Guidance

One of the Prophet's key instructions was to confirm each verse's placement right after its revelation. He would say, "These verses belong in Surah so-and-so, after the verses that mention such-and-such." This directive gave clarity, preventing scribes from guessing the surah's sequence themselves. Because he was alive and actively guiding them, any discrepancies in wording or arrangement could be addressed immediately. The Prophet's authority in this matter prevented the confusion of variant texts that might otherwise have emerged.

7.4 Memorization: The Core Method of Preservation

7.4.1 Cultural Tradition of Oral Transmission

Arab society in the 7th century was known for its strong oral tradition. Poets memorized lengthy compositions, recited them at fairs, and passed them down through generations without relying heavily on written manuscripts. When the Quran was revealed, it took advantage of this cultural strength. The rhythmic style, distinctive structure, and eloquent language made it easier to commit to memory.

7.4.2 Hufadh (Memorizers) of the Quran

Believers who memorized the Quran in its entirety or significant portions became known as "Hafiz" (plural "Huffadh"). Many companions achieved this status, including Abdullah ibn Mas'ud, Salim Mawla Abi Hudhayfah, and Ubayy ibn Ka'b. By repeatedly reciting in congregational prayers and private study, they preserved the text down to each word and syllable.

The Prophet encouraged memorization not just for spiritual reward but also as a practical means of safeguarding God's word. In an era where physical materials could be damaged or lost, having human beings carry the text in their minds was a reliable form of preservation. Should a written copy go missing, the Huffadh could instantly restore the content from memory.

7.4.3 Regular Review and Public Recitation

Memorizers did not merely store the verses in their minds; they reviewed them frequently—often daily. Recitations in the mosque allowed the community to hear the Quran together, ensuring that any accidental changes would be corrected on the spot. This public process acted like a living quality control system. If someone drifted from the precise wording, others would correct them, maintaining uniformity across the community.

Additionally, the Prophet would sometimes ask certain companions to recite the Quran aloud to him. In these sessions, he confirmed their memorization and also used the recitation as an opportunity to convey deeper insights or context for the verses. This direct interaction reinforced the idea that the Quran was meant to be both learned and lived.

7.5 The Annual Review with Jibril

7.5.1 Ramadan Sessions

A well-known tradition states that every Ramadan, the Angel Jibril would meet the Prophet to review the Quran revealed thus far. They would recite it together, ensuring all verses were in their correct order. This practice provided a divine audit of sorts, reaffirming that no human error had crept into the text.

Companions like Ibn Abbas and Fatimah reported that the Prophet took these review sessions very seriously. He might spend extended nights in worship, recitation, and reflection, aligning his heart and memory with the revealed words. In the final Ramadan before his death, the Prophet reviewed the Quran with Jibril twice. Some companions interpreted this double review as a sign that his mission was nearing completion.

7.5.2 The Last Review as a Sign of Completion

That last review was significant: it indicated that the Quran, as a revealed text, was nearing its final form. After it ended, only a few verses were revealed. Many companions noticed that the Prophet's health began to decline in the months following that Ramadan, and they saw the double review as divine preparation for the Prophet's passing. By cross-checking all verses, the Quran reached a state of completion under the direct supervision of the Prophet, leaving no ambiguity about its contents.

7.6 Specific Companions Known for Mastery of the Quran

7.6.1 Ubayy ibn Ka'b

Ubayy ibn Ka'b was renowned among the Ansar (the Helpers in Medina) for his deep knowledge of the Quran. The Prophet once called him "the leader of the reciters" (Sayyid al-Qurra). Ubayy had a strong memory and served as a frequent reference if other companions questioned a verse's exact wording. His devotion to preserving the text was well-known, and he served as a scribe when needed.

7.6.2 Abdullah ibn Mas'ud

Originally from Mecca, Abdullah ibn Mas'ud embraced Islam early. He possessed a beautiful voice and profound understanding of the Quran, shaped by close association with the Prophet. Ibn Mas'ud's recitations moved many to tears, and he was often consulted on matters of interpretation and the correct reading of verses.

7.6.3 Zayd ibn Thabit

As mentioned earlier, Zayd ibn Thabit took a leading role in writing the Quran during the Medinan period. Later, he would also head the post-Prophetic compilation efforts. His meticulous approach and close contact with the Prophet made him a trusted figure for verifying verses. Zayd's literacy, intelligence, and calm demeanor suited him well for the task of overseeing the written preservation of scripture.

7.6.4 Ali ibn Abi Talib

Although revered for his leadership and knowledge in many areas, Ali ibn Abi Talib also wrote verses under the Prophet's guidance. He possessed a deep grasp of the Quran's teachings and is widely cited for his theological insights. After the Prophet's passing, Ali continued to instruct believers in correct recitation and interpretation, building on his experiences from the Prophet's lifetime.

7.7 Partial Collections Before the Prophet's Passing

7.7.1 Private Codices

Some companions kept private collections of written verses for their personal reference. These codices were not complete copies of the entire Quran in a single bound volume, but rather a gathering of surahs or portions that each companion found most relevant. There might have been slight differences in the arrangement or inclusion of notes explaining contexts. These personal codices helped many to learn and teach others, although the community as a whole relied heavily on memorization.

7.7.2 Careful Organization

Despite the presence of these smaller collections, the Prophet never asked for one single, official manuscript to be produced and distributed. The living presence of so many memorizers, plus multiple scribes writing in parallel, made the risk of losing the Quran minimal during his lifetime. Additionally, revelations continued until shortly before his death, so the text was not "finalized" in terms of new verses until then.

7.7.3 The Absence of a Bound, Single Codex

A reason often cited for the absence of a single compiled codex during the Prophet's life was that revelation was ongoing. Another reason was that the companions did not use bound books in the modern sense. Scrolls or various sheets were more common. Also, the Prophet had the authority to resolve any confusion directly. When he passed away, however, the need for a more systematic, centralized collection became pressing—since no new verses would be revealed, and the guiding presence of the Prophet was no longer there to clarify variations or disputes.

7.8 The Prophet's Assurance of Preservation

7.8.1 Divine Guarantee

The Quran itself contains verses indicating that God would protect it from corruption (for example, Quran 15:9: "Indeed, it is We who sent down the Quran and indeed, We will be its guardian"). The Prophet reiterated this promise, reassuring believers that the text would remain intact for future generations. This divine promise motivated companions to handle the revealed words with great care.

7.8.2 The Prophet's Oral Confirmations

Throughout the final years of his life, the Prophet repeatedly emphasized the importance of adhering to the Quran. In various sermons and personal instructions, he would remind Muslims to learn and teach its verses. He cautioned them never to neglect the revelation or twist its meaning. These statements set the tone for the companions' reverence and sense of responsibility.

7.8.3 Maintaining Unity

The Prophet stressed that the Quran was a source of unity among believers, transcending tribal and geographic boundaries. He warned them not to dispute over its interpretation in a way that would create divisions. Rather, the Quran was meant to serve as a moral and spiritual foundation for the expanding ummah (community). This sense of unity around the text would become crucial during later disagreements that arose after the Prophet's death.

7.9 The Final Months and Continuing Revelations

7.9.1 Indications of the Mission's Completion

By the tenth year after the migration (circa 632 CE), signs indicated that the Prophet's mission was nearing completion. Many Arabian tribes had either embraced Islam or formed peaceful agreements with the Muslim community in Medina. Revelations addressing essential legal and social matters had been largely delivered, and the Prophet's final pilgrimage that year further demonstrated that Islam was now firmly rooted in the Arabian Peninsula.

7.9.2 The Verse Indicating Completion

A verse often linked to the near-end of revelations is found in Surah Al-Ma'idah (5:3): "Today I have perfected for you your religion and completed My favor upon you and have approved for you Islam as religion." Tradition holds that this verse came down during the Farewell Pilgrimage. The Prophet reportedly sensed that with this statement, the core of Islam's teachings were now established. Only a few verses were revealed after this, addressing specific circumstances.

7.9.3 Ongoing Efforts Until the End

Even in his last days, the Prophet remained vigilant about preserving the Quran. If any new verses were revealed, he instructed scribes to record them properly and ensured key memorizers learned them. Despite declining health, his dedication to maintaining the integrity of the revelation did not wane. This continuous vigilance was a testament to the central place the Quran held in Islamic life.

Chapter Eight: The Farewell Sermon and the Last Revelations

8.1 Introduction

In the tenth year after the Hijrah (around 632 CE), the Prophet Muhammad made the journey from Medina to Mecca to perform what would become known as the Farewell Pilgrimage. This event was more than a simple religious rite. It was the culmination of a decades-long mission that transformed the Arabian Peninsula. During this pilgrimage, the Prophet addressed a large gathering of Muslims in what is traditionally called the "Farewell Sermon." These words highlighted core teachings of Islam, stressed social justice, and reminded believers to stay united under the guidance of the Quran.

Shortly after the Farewell Pilgrimage, a few final verses were revealed, offering last instructions and clarifications for the Muslim community. Then, within months, the Prophet fell ill and passed away. This chapter details the events of the Farewell Pilgrimage, examines the key points of the Farewell Sermon, and explores how the last revelations fit into the broader message of the Quran. We will also look at the Prophet's final days and the immediate impact of his death on the Muslim community. Through these events, we see how the Quran and the

Prophet's teachings were solidified in the hearts of believers, ready to be carried forth without his physical presence.

8.2 Preparations for the Farewell Pilgrimage

8.2.1 Call to the Believers

In the early part of the tenth year after the Hijrah, the Prophet announced his intention to perform Hajj. By now, most of Arabia was under Muslim influence, and many tribes had embraced Islam. Word spread quickly that the Prophet would be leading the pilgrimage. Thousands answered the call, traveling from distant regions to join him.

For many, this would be the first time performing Hajj under Islamic rituals, free from the idol worship that once pervaded the Ka'bah. The Prophet took care to explain the proper procedures, ensuring the pilgrims understood each step as an act of worship to the one God. Camels and other livestock were prepared for sacrifice, and the caravan from Medina set out with excitement and reverence.

8.2.2 The Journey to Mecca

The route from Medina to Mecca took over a week by camel. Along the way, the Prophet led prayers and gave short talks, reminding the pilgrims of their obligations to God and to one another. The mood was celebratory, yet solemn. Many pilgrims realized that this might be the last time they would perform Hajj with the Prophet himself.

By this time in his life, the Prophet was in his early sixties. Though still actively guiding the community, some companions noticed signs of his fatigue. His hair had grayed, and he occasionally leaned on a staff for support. Yet his resolve remained firm—he wanted to demonstrate the final form of the pilgrimage rituals, aligning them fully with monotheistic worship.

8.2.3 Arrival in Mecca and Cleansing of Idols

When the Muslims arrived in Mecca, they found the city peacefully under their influence. The conquest of Mecca two years prior had removed idols from the

Ka'bah. The sanctuary was now devoted to the worship of the one God, just as Prophet Abraham had originally intended. The Prophet and his companions entered the holy precinct, reciting praises to God. Over the next few days, they performed the Tawaf (circling of the Ka'bah), the Sa'i (walking between the hills of Safa and Marwah), and other rites that formed the core of the Hajj.

8.3 The Main Elements of the Farewell Pilgrimage

8.3.1 Standing at Arafat

One of the key moments of the pilgrimage is the Wuquf, or "standing" at the plain of Arafat. This ritual symbolizes the believers' gathering on the Day of Judgment, seeking God's mercy. On the ninth day of the Islamic month of Dhu al-Hijjah, the Prophet stood among the thousands of pilgrims on Arafat, offering supplications. He recited passages from the Quran and delivered important guidance. Some accounts say that part of Surah Al-Ma'idah (5:3) was revealed there, declaring that God had "perfected your religion and completed My favor upon you."

8.3.2 The Sermon at Mount Arafat

Although historical records differ slightly on the exact location and timing, most versions indicate that the Prophet delivered a seminal address at or near Arafat. He stood before the assembled crowd, which included men and women from various tribes and backgrounds. His voice carried across the plain, or was relayed by individuals who repeated his words so everyone could hear. This sermon addressed fundamental principles:

1. **Sanctity of Life and Property**: He declared that the blood and property of every Muslim are inviolable, likening their sacredness to the holiness of Mecca itself.
2. **Equality of All Believers**: He emphasized that no Arab is superior to a non-Arab, nor a non-Arab to an Arab, and no white person is superior to a black person, nor black person to a white person. Righteousness alone defines a person's worth in God's sight.

3. **Rights of Women**: He reminded men to treat women kindly, recognizing their rights within marriage and society.
4. **Prohibition of Usury and Vengeance**: He canceled all outstanding usurious transactions and told the community to abandon the cycle of vengeance from pre-Islamic times.
5. **Adherence to the Quran**: He urged believers to hold fast to the Quran (and, in some narrations, his Sunnah—his example), to avoid straying from the path of guidance.

8.3.3 Symbolic End of the Pre-Islamic Era

In this sermon, the Prophet signaled the end of many pre-Islamic customs that fueled injustice and discord. He declared that the new Islamic social order was based on fairness, brotherhood, and devotion to God. By doing so on the day of Arafat, in the presence of a massive gathering, the Prophet ensured that these directives reached a broad audience. People who attended could carry the message back to their tribes, spreading the final teachings throughout Arabia.

8.4 Key Messages of the Farewell Sermon

8.4.1 Sanctity and Justice

The Prophet's sermon stressed that the life, property, and honor of each believer should be protected. This was a radical shift from the tribal culture that often justified raids, blood feuds, and vendettas. By linking the sanctity of human life to the sanctity of the sacred month and the holy city, he raised moral standards beyond local custom or personal grudges.

8.4.2 Abolishing Economic Exploitation

Usury (riba) was a common practice in pre-Islamic Arabia, causing debtors to sink into ever deeper financial enslavement. The Prophet declared all interest-based debts null. This measure tackled one of the main sources of economic oppression. By removing the exploitation of the poor, Islam aimed to establish a more just financial system.

8.4.3 Mutual Rights and Responsibilities

The Prophet instructed men to remember that they had taken their wives in trust from God. In return, wives were expected to maintain fidelity and companionship. This balanced framework recognized the dignity of women and underscored that marriage was a partnership with reciprocal obligations. The sermon thereby challenged the norms that left women vulnerable to abuse or neglect.

8.4.4 Brotherhood and Unity

Unity was a central theme. The Prophet cautioned believers not to revert to rivalries and conflicts of the pre-Islamic period. Under Islam, all racial, ethnic, and tribal distinctions took a back seat to the common bond of faith. This message resonated in a region long plagued by tribal warfare, opening the door for peaceful coexistence and cooperation across diverse groups.

8.5 Revelation of Surah Al-Ma'idah (5:3)

8.5.1 "Today I Have Perfected Your Religion"

Many companions recall that while at Arafat, the following verse was revealed:

> "This day I have perfected for you your religion and completed My favor upon you and have approved for you Islam as religion." (Quran 5:3)

This verse signaled a milestone. According to numerous reports, some companions wept with joy and sadness, sensing that the Prophet's mission was approaching completion. They realized that if the religion was perfected, there might not be much time left with the Prophet.

8.5.2 Implications of Completion

The completion of the religion meant that core doctrines, moral guidelines, and social legislation were all established. Remaining revelations would clarify certain issues, but the foundation was set. Islam had matured from a small community surviving persecution in Mecca to a broad-based society with established laws in Medina—and now overshadowed all of Arabia. The verse reassured believers that the message was intact and would guide future generations even in the Prophet's absence.

8.6 After Arafat: Eid al-Adha and Other Rites

8.6.1 The Sacrifice and Celebration

Following the Day of Arafat, pilgrims moved to Muzdalifah for a night's rest and devotion, then proceeded to Mina to perform the symbolic stoning of pillars representing evil. They also sacrificed animals (camels, sheep, or goats), a tradition tracing back to Prophet Abraham's willingness to offer his son in obedience to God. This ritual of sacrifice is commemorated as Eid al-Adha, a festival of gratitude where meat is distributed to the poor.

8.6.2 Final Tawaf and Completion of Hajj

Pilgrims returned to Mecca to perform a farewell circumambulation (Tawaf al-Wida'), signifying the completion of their Hajj. The Prophet stayed in Mecca for several more days, teaching final details of the pilgrimage rituals to ensure that future generations could replicate them accurately. He then left Mecca, accompanied by the thousands who had shared in this historic journey.

8.6.3 Widespread Dissemination of the Message

Those who witnessed the Farewell Pilgrimage carried its lessons back to their tribes. Many had recorded or memorized the Prophet's words, especially the sermon's highlights. As a result, the principles declared at Arafat—justice, equality, the sanctity of life, and adherence to the Quran—spread rapidly across the Arabian Peninsula. In the months following the pilgrimage, the unity among Muslims strengthened, and conversions continued among some remaining pockets of idolatry.

8.7 The Last Revelations

8.7.1 Verses After the Farewell Pilgrimage

Although Surah Al-Ma'idah (5:3) indicated the religion's completion, a few more verses were revealed in the weeks and months that followed. These final passages addressed ongoing situations, such as clarifications on inheritance, reminders to uphold justice, or instructions related to vows and oaths. One example is found in Surah At-Tawbah (9:128-129), though scholars differ on the exact chronology. The Prophet continued to guide scribes to record these verses in their proper places within the surahs.

8.7.2 The Prophet's Illness

Towards the end of the eleventh month of the Islamic calendar or soon after, the Prophet's health began to decline. Some traditions suggest that he suffered from a high fever and headaches. Despite the pain, he still led prayers at the mosque until his condition worsened. During this time, he occasionally imparted short advices, urging Muslims to remain steadfast, avoid division, and hold fast to the Quran.

8.7.3 Reassurances and Final Words

During his final illness, the Prophet spent much of his time in Aisha's chamber, one of the small rooms adjacent to the mosque. Many companions gathered anxiously outside, hoping for updates on his condition. On one occasion, when he felt slightly better, he delivered a brief address at the mosque, reminding believers of the importance of prayer and fair treatment of those under their care, such as servants and subordinates. Those were among the last public words he spoke, reflecting his lifelong concern for justice and piety.

8.8 The Prophet's Death

8.8.1 Passing Away in Aisha's Arms

The Prophet passed away in early June 632 CE (Rabi' al-Awwal 11 AH) in the arms of his wife, Aisha. His final moments included whispered prayers. According to some accounts, he spoke softly about joining "the Highest Companion," referring to God. When the news spread through Medina, many companions were stunned, unable to accept that their guide and leader was gone. Some, like Umar ibn al-Khattab, initially refused to believe the Prophet was truly dead.

8.8.2 Abu Bakr's Calm Announcement

Abu Bakr, the Prophet's closest companion and friend, entered Aisha's room, confirmed the Prophet's passing, and then addressed the people. He famously said, "If anyone worshiped Muhammad, let them know that Muhammad is dead. But if anyone worshiped God, know that God is alive and never dies." This statement calmed the uproar, reminding everyone that the Prophet was a human messenger and that the revelation he brought—namely the Quran—remained as the lasting guide.

8.8.3 Collective Grief and Immediate Concerns

In the hours after the Prophet's death, believers grieved deeply. The city of Medina fell silent in mourning. Practical matters also arose quickly: the community needed to select a leader to handle governance and unify the Muslims. Additionally, people began to reflect on how best to preserve the Prophet's teachings, especially as new challenges would arise without his direct presence.

8.9 The Quran's Role After the Prophet's Death

8.9.1 A Completed Scripture

With the Prophet's passing, the revelation ceased. The Quran now existed in a completed form: memorized by many, partially written by scribes, and scattered in various materials. The immediate need was to gather these pieces into a single, authoritative text to prevent any future confusion. That task, however, would be undertaken under the leadership of the first caliph, Abu Bakr, and continued by subsequent caliphs.

8.9.2 Fulfillment of the Farewell Sermon's Directives

Even in the immediate weeks after the Prophet's death, the community strived to honor the instructions from the Farewell Sermon. Tribal feuds were discouraged, women's rights gradually improved in practice, and a sense of equality among believers grew. While not every social transformation was instantaneous, the blueprint provided by the Prophet's last major address helped shape the young Islamic society's direction.

8.9.3 Source of Unity and Reference

Amid uncertainties about leadership and the challenges of expansion, the Quran offered a constant point of reference. Companions turned to its verses for guidance on governance, interpersonal disputes, and moral dilemmas. The text that the Prophet had so carefully preserved through memorization, scribes, and recitation was now the main guiding source.

8.10 The Impact of the Farewell Sermon on Future Generations

8.10.1 Upholding Equality

The Prophet's call for an end to racism and tribal supremacy laid a foundation for future generations. Although social hierarchies continued in various forms, the principle of universal brotherhood and equality influenced Islamic lawmaking, scholarship, and governance over centuries. Whenever injustices arose, reformers often cited the Farewell Sermon, reminding rulers and citizens alike that Islam's original teachings demanded equity.

8.10.2 Moral Economy

The prohibition of usury and the focus on fair transactions shaped the economic ethics of the early caliphs. While actual implementation varied, these guidelines left a lasting impression on how Islamic law dealt with contracts, loans, and business dealings. The idea that wealth should serve the community's well-being, rather than exploit the vulnerable, remains a hallmark of Islamic economic thought.

8.10.3 Women's Rights and Family Structure

By underscoring women's rights in marriage and the importance of treating wives kindly, the Farewell Sermon introduced transformative concepts to a patriarchal society. Although progress was neither uniform nor immediate, the Prophet's words equipped Muslim jurists and families with principles to advocate for better treatment of women. Over time, these ideals became woven into Islamic discourse on marriage and gender relations.

8.11 Lessons from the Final Revelations

8.11.1 Adherence to Divine Guidance

The last verses revealed demonstrated that even with a comprehensive religion, believers would continue to face new situations. They needed to anchor themselves in the Quran's timeless moral framework. The revelation consistently urged them to consult God's commands, seek knowledge, and strive for righteousness in every aspect of life.

8.11.2 Endurance of Divine Promise

The Quran had promised to remain protected. The Prophet's demise did not undermine this guarantee; if anything, it underscored it. Although new revelations would no longer descend, the text was already safely embedded in the hearts of believers and in scattered written forms. Future generations would rely on the companions—who had personally witnessed the revelation process—to confirm and compile the Quran in its final written format.

8.11.3 The Prophet's Example as a Lasting Guide

While the Farewell Sermon reiterated the primacy of the Quran, it also pointed to the Prophet's example (Sunnah) as a vital reference. Many instructions—such as how to perform the Hajj rituals or specific details of moral conduct—came from the Prophet's actions and explanations. Over time, scholars compiled these sayings and traditions into collections of Hadith, forming a second source of Islamic teachings. Alongside the Quran, this body of traditions guided believers on questions the Quran did not address explicitly.

Chapter Nine: The Preservation of the Quran After the Prophet's Death

9.1 Introduction

The passing of Prophet Muhammad in 632 CE was a moment of profound grief for the Muslim community. For more than two decades, the revelation of the Quran had guided them through persecution, migration, social reform, and the eventual unification of much of the Arabian Peninsula. With the Prophet's demise, no more revelations would descend; the holy text was now considered complete.

However, the immediate challenge confronting the companions (Sahabah) was how to preserve the Quran's authenticity going forward. While the Prophet had ensured that many people memorized the Quran, and that verses were written on different materials, there was no single, bound manuscript containing the entire text. The community faced new internal and external pressures that could risk the loss or alteration of precious verses. This chapter explores the steps taken in the immediate aftermath of the Prophet's death, the role of key companions in preserving the Quran's integrity, and the circumstances that led to discussions about formally compiling the holy text into one collection.

9.2 Immediate Challenges Following the Prophet's Death

9.2.1 Grief and Shock in the Community

When news spread that the Prophet had passed away, Medina was overwhelmed by a wave of disbelief and sorrow. Many companions had lived through great trials with him—exile from Mecca, battles for survival, and remarkable social changes. They struggled to imagine life without their beloved leader and the direct source of divine revelation. Although the Quran was complete, questions arose on how to maintain unity and address new disputes without the Prophet's immediate guidance.

9.2.2 Leadership Vacuum and Succession

Within hours of the Prophet's death, prominent companions, including Abu Bakr and Umar, recognized the urgency of appointing a new leader to unify the Muslim community. Several Ansar (the Helpers in Medina) met at the Saqifah (a covered courtyard) to discuss who should succeed the Prophet as a political and administrative leader, though not as a prophet. After deliberations, Abu Bakr was chosen as the first caliph (khalifah), a term meaning "successor" in the sense of stewardship over the community. This swift appointment prevented deeper divisions that could have jeopardized the nascent Muslim polity.

9.2.3 The Impulse to Preserve Guidance

Amid these rapid political shifts, the companions clung to the Quran as the permanent, unchanging source of divine instruction. Many understood that the Prophet had meticulously overseen the memorization and partial documentation of each revealed verse. Now, with him gone, any further clarifications or recitations could not be verified directly by the Prophet. The Quran was complete, but ensuring that every single syllable remained accurately transmitted became a paramount concern.

9.3 Existing Preservation Methods at the Time of the Prophet's Passing

9.3.1 Memorization by Huffadh

By the time of the Prophet's death, scores of companions—known as Huffadh (sing. Hafiz)—had committed the entire Quran to memory. Even more had memorized substantial portions. This oral preservation was deeply embedded in the Arabian culture, which prized poetry recitation and strong memory. The Prophet had encouraged memorization both for spiritual reward and as a practical safeguard.

Muslims regularly recited the Quran in their daily prayers, nighttime devotions, and communal gatherings. This repetitive recitation helped fix the verses in their minds. If anyone erred during a public recitation, multiple listeners could correct them on the spot. This collective vigilance served as a living "quality control" mechanism, reducing the chances of introducing mistakes.

9.3.2 Written Fragments and Materials

In addition to memorization, several scribes wrote down verses on available materials. These included parchment, leather, palm leaves, stones, bones (like flat shoulder blades of camels or sheep), and pieces of cloth. While advanced papermaking had not yet reached Arabia in significant quantity, some papyrus might have been imported from neighboring regions. Quality parchment was more common among wealthier individuals.

These writings were not compiled into a single codex during the Prophet's lifetime. Instead, many companions kept partial collections for personal study and teaching. Because new verses continued to be revealed until the Prophet's final days, standardizing a single manuscript was not a priority at that time; the Prophet himself oversaw the correct placement of newly revealed passages within existing surahs.

9.3.3 Annual Review with the Prophet

A major factor ensuring accurate preservation was the Prophet's annual review of the Quran with the Angel Jibril each Ramadan. In the final year of his life, he underwent this review twice, suggesting to many that his time was near.

Although the companions could no longer witness these sessions after his death, the memory of them provided confidence that the revealed text, in the arrangement the Prophet had directed, was indeed complete and precise.

9.4 Early Concerns About Potential Loss

9.4.1 Transition into a Period of Turmoil

Immediately following the Prophet's passing, the newly formed caliphate faced a crisis known as the Ridda (apostasy) Wars. Certain tribes in Arabia either stopped paying zakat (the mandatory charity) or renounced Islam altogether, claiming their allegiance was to Muhammad personally, not to Abu Bakr or any institutionalized faith. The community had to mobilize militarily to preserve the unity and authority of the fledgling Islamic state.

With multiple battles and skirmishes looming, there was a rising concern that many of those who had memorized large portions of the Quran could be killed in combat. If that happened, valuable oral knowledge might vanish with them, especially if they were key memorizers of certain passages. The potential for such a loss spurred some companions to question whether the time had come to compile the Quran in a more permanent form.

9.4.2 Reports of Casualties Among Huffadh

In the early skirmishes that broke out during the Ridda Wars, there were reports of experienced reciters and memorizers of the Quran dying in battle. While the total numbers remain subject to various historical accounts, the sense of alarm grew. Umar ibn al-Khattab, a leading companion, became notably concerned that these losses could lead to significant gaps in the oral transmission if not promptly addressed.

9.4.3 Urgency to Protect the Text from Fragmentation

The Muslim community was expanding geographically, and new converts often relied on local teachers who had memorized or written portions of the Quran. If such teachers were lost, or if partial manuscripts fell into disuse, the possibility of minor textual differences or even accidental omissions arose. While memorization remained robust, the community recognized that a more systematic approach would ensure the entire Quran, as revealed to the Prophet, remained absolutely intact.

9.5 The Role of Key Companions in Preservation

9.5.1 Abu Bakr's Administrative Responsibilities

Abu Bakr, now the first caliph, had to balance multiple priorities: quelling rebellions, maintaining internal stability, and safeguarding the integrity of Islamic teachings. Though he personally had strong faith in the reliability of the memorizers and the partial written records, he understood that circumstances had changed drastically since the Prophet's lifetime. As the recognized leader, he bore ultimate responsibility for the community's spiritual welfare.

9.5.2 Umar ibn al-Khattab's Persuasion

Umar, who would later become the second caliph, took a more proactive stance. He argued that relying solely on dispersed memorization and fragmentary manuscripts was risky in a time of warfare. Umar approached Abu Bakr with the idea of gathering all existing verses into one unified codex. Initially, Abu Bakr hesitated, recalling that the Prophet himself had not assembled a single manuscript. However, Umar pressed that the context had changed and that preserving the Quran in one volume was now a necessary measure to avert the risk of partial loss.

9.5.3 Consultation with Other Senior Companions

Abu Bakr sought input from other eminent companions, including members of the Prophet's immediate household (Ahl al-Bayt) and senior scribes like Ubayy ibn Ka'b, Ali ibn Abi Talib, and Zayd ibn Thabit. The consensus formed that no new revelation would appear, and the Prophet was no longer present to resolve any minor transcription issues. Thus, a carefully managed compilation seemed the prudent course of action.

9.6 Early Discussions on Compilation

9.6.1 Debate Over Innovation (Bid'ah)

A major point of debate was whether compiling the Quran in a single manuscript constituted an innovation (bid'ah), a concept frowned upon in Islamic theology if it contradicts or adds to the religion. Abu Bakr initially argued that the Prophet never undertook such a task, so doing it now might be unwarranted. Umar and other supporters countered that the Prophet's decision was shaped by continuous revelation and his direct oversight. With no further revelation forthcoming and the Prophet absent, the circumstances had shifted, making a formal compilation a necessary preservation effort rather than an unwelcome innovation.

9.6.2 The Principle of Maslahah (Public Interest)

Faced with the question of preserving the Quran's authenticity, many companions invoked the principle of maslahah (public interest or welfare), suggesting that ensuring the safety of the sacred text was paramount. The risk of losing verses due to the deaths of Huffadh or the scattering of written fragments was deemed a far greater danger than any perceived innovation. By framing the compilation as a safeguarding measure, the community found religious legitimacy in the plan.

9.6.3 The Prophet's Example of Adaptation

During his lifetime, the Prophet had adapted several practices in response to new conditions—changing the direction of prayer (Qiblah) from Jerusalem to Mecca, gradually prohibiting alcohol, and so forth. These transformations were guided by ongoing revelation, yes, but they also illustrated how Islam was prepared to address evolving circumstances. Now, in the absence of revelation, reasoned decisions by the community's leadership could likewise address urgent needs, provided they did not conflict with established Islamic principles.

9.7 Emphasis on Oral Verification and Witnesses

9.7.1 Community-Based Confirmation

One method proposed was to require that each verse included in the compilation must be confirmed by multiple witnesses: those who had memorized the verse and those who possessed written evidence. This approach would ensure that no single individual's memory or personal manuscript introduced a variant reading. Instead, a communal process would validate each segment of text.

9.7.2 Organized Cross-Referencing

Because the community included many Huffadh who had memorized the Quran directly under the Prophet's supervision, cross-referencing could resolve any discrepancies. If, for instance, a verse was found on a piece of parchment but lacked a second corroborating source, it would need to be verified by at least two memorizers who had heard it directly from the Prophet or recited it under his guidance. This robust verification process took time and effort but aimed to eliminate the slightest possibility of error.

9.7.3 Avoiding Reliance on a Single Companion's Codex

Some companions, such as Ubayy ibn Ka'b and Ibn Mas'ud, had private codices that covered most or all of the Quran. Nonetheless, the leadership decided that the official compilation must not rely exclusively on any individual's text. Instead, every verse had to be traced back to multiple sources, reflecting the communal nature of the Quran's preservation. This principle avoided giving undue authority to one companion's personal collection.

9.8 Seeds of the Official Compilation

9.8.1 Abu Bakr's Decision

After thorough discussions, prayer, and reflection, Abu Bakr concluded that preserving the Quran in a single manuscript was both necessary and legitimate. He understood that while the Prophet had not undertaken this task personally, the changing circumstances justified it. This decision marked a historic turning point in the history of the Quran, laying the groundwork for a written standard that would guide future generations.

9.8.2 Zayd ibn Thabit's Emerging Role

Zayd ibn Thabit, a young but highly respected companion, was already recognized for his expertise in writing and memorizing the Quran. He had been a primary scribe for the Prophet in Medina. Given his skill, integrity, and close association with revelation, he was the natural choice to lead the practical work of collecting and verifying scattered verses. Umar ibn al-Khattab was also deeply involved, supporting Zayd's efforts with his own zeal for preserving the text.

9.8.3 The Influence of the Ridda Wars

Simultaneously, the Ridda Wars were ongoing, requiring military campaigns to bring rebellious tribes back into the Islamic fold. This period of instability heightened the sense of urgency. Zayd's assignment to gather the Quran was not a mere scholarly exercise; it was a decisive action to protect the core religious text at a time when some of its staunchest keepers risked martyrdom in battle.

Chapter Ten: Caliph Abu Bakr's Era and the First Official Collection

10.1 Introduction

When Abu Bakr assumed the caliphate, he inherited a community united by faith but fraught with challenges, including political uncertainty, military threats from rebellious tribes, and the pressing need to safeguard the Quran. Despite the turmoil, Abu Bakr's leadership proved instrumental in ensuring that the scripture—now complete but dispersed in the memories of individuals and across various written fragments—would not become fragmented itself.

In this chapter, we examine how Abu Bakr led the historic endeavor to collect the Quran into a formal manuscript. We explore the impetus behind the project (the Ridda Wars), the selection of Zayd ibn Thabit as the chief compiler, the rigorous methodology for verifying verses, and the final outcome of this pioneering compilation. The thoroughness of this first official collection laid the foundation for the standardized Quranic text, ensuring that the word of God remained unchanged through the centuries ahead.

10.2 Caliph Abu Bakr's Leadership Context

10.2.1 Stabilizing a Fractured Arabia

Upon the Prophet's death, several tribes questioned their obligations to the new central authority in Medina. Some claimed they owed no zakat, while others declared outright independence. Referred to historically as the Ridda Wars, these conflicts threatened to unravel the unity painstakingly built under the Prophet. Abu Bakr stood firm, insisting that Islam was not tied to the Prophet as an individual but remained binding upon believers even after his death.

As small wars flared across the Arabian Peninsula, Abu Bakr organized and dispatched armies led by seasoned companions, including Khalid ibn al-Walid, to subdue rebel tribes. These campaigns succeeded in restoring most of Arabia to the Islamic fold, but at a cost in lives. Among those killed were individuals who had memorized large portions of the Quran (Huffadh), intensifying the fear that the text could be endangered if more memorizers perished.

10.2.2 Reinforcing Islamic Practice and Learning

Even while organizing military campaigns, Abu Bakr took steps to keep religious education active in Medina. Mosques in various regions continued to offer Quranic instruction. Envoys carrying the Prophet's teachings were sent to distant tribes, clarifying that the message of Islam remained the same. The trust in the Quran as a divine guide became the unifying thread that bound believers from different tribes and regions.

10.2.3 Umar's Influence in Preserving the Quran

Umar ibn al-Khattab, the future second caliph, strongly supported Abu Bakr. He recognized that in the absence of new revelations, preserving the existing text was paramount. Umar had already raised the issue of compilation when he approached Abu Bakr, pointing out the potential danger of losing sections of the Quran if more Huffadh died in battle. His persistent advocacy contributed to Abu Bakr's resolve to initiate the official collection project.

10.3 The Impetus for the Official Collection: The Ridda Wars

10.3.1 Battles and the Loss of Memorizers

As the Ridda Wars raged, pockets of heavy fighting erupted in regions such as Yamamah, where Musaylimah the Liar (a false claimant to prophethood) challenged the Medinan authority. In these battles, a number of the Prophet's companions—some of them distinguished Huffadh—were martyred. Although precise numbers vary in historical records, the community's concern skyrocketed upon hearing that well-known reciters had been killed.

10.3.2 The Risk of Fragmentation

The fear was not necessarily that entire surahs would vanish overnight, but that small nuances in certain verses could be lost or disputed over time if key witnesses died. Oral transmission was robust, but reliance on the memories of a diminishing group carried risks, especially as Islam expanded and new teachers had fewer direct connections to the Prophet's era. Ensuring a stable reference text began to seem indispensable.

10.3.3 Calls to Action

News from the battlefield reached Medina: accounts of heroic last stands by faithful reciters who refused to abandon their duty, but also the grim reality of high casualties. Umar repeatedly appealed to Abu Bakr, arguing that while the Prophet had not compiled the Quran in a single volume, present circumstances were unprecedented. The only way to maintain uniformity and completeness was to assemble a carefully verified manuscript. Abu Bakr, after initial hesitation, saw the wisdom in Umar's counsel.

10.4 Commissioning Zayd ibn Thabit

10.4.1 Qualifications of Zayd ibn Thabit

Abu Bakr's next step was selecting someone with impeccable credentials to oversee the compilation process. Zayd ibn Thabit stood out:

1. **Close Association with the Prophet**: He had served as one of the main scribes in Medina, writing down verses under the Prophet's direct supervision.
2. **Memorizer of the Quran**: Zayd was himself a Hafiz, having memorized the text.
3. **Proven Integrity**: Known for his diligence and reliability, Zayd commanded respect among the companions.

Recognizing these attributes, Abu Bakr appointed Zayd to lead the collection effort, with Umar as a key advisor and the broader community as participants in verification.

10.4.2 Zayd's Initial Hesitation

Zayd expressed reluctance when first tasked with the job. His reverence for the Prophet's example led him to question how they could embark on something the Prophet had not explicitly done. Echoing Abu Bakr's initial doubts, Zayd worried about inadvertently introducing an error. However, Umar and Abu Bakr reassured him that this was not an unwarranted innovation but a necessary preservation effort, fully in line with the Quranic command to protect divine revelation.

10.4.3 Official Mandate

With his scruples addressed, Zayd accepted the commission. Abu Bakr granted him the authority to collect every verse from across the community, cross-check multiple oral and written sources, and compile them into a single, cohesive manuscript. Zayd gathered a team of reliable companions to assist in the extensive task of collecting, organizing, and verifying the text.

10.5 Methodology of Verification

10.5.1 Public Announcement

One of Zayd's first moves was to make a public call in Medina and its surrounding regions: any companion who had written fragments of the Quran, or memorized portions, should come forward to participate in the verification process. This wide invitation ensured that the compilation would not rely on a narrow set of manuscripts or individuals.

10.5.2 Dual Evidence Requirement

Based on the protocol established in consultations with Abu Bakr and Umar, a verse would only be accepted into the compiled manuscript if it met two conditions:

1. **Written Documentation**: A physical fragment bearing the verse, usually recognized by others as authentic.
2. **Oral Testimony**: At least two reliable witnesses who had memorized the verse directly from the Prophet (or from a chain that directly traced back to him).

This approach mirrored the legal principle that significant claims require corroboration to avoid mistakes. In effect, the compilation served as a meticulous "trial" for each verse, ensuring only verified passages were admitted.

10.5.3 Resolving Minor Variants

If any discrepancy arose—for example, if two companions remembered a slight difference in wording—Zayd and his aides would refer to the largest pool of memorizers, or to senior scribes who had recorded the text under the Prophet's instruction. Given that the Prophet had personally overseen the arrangement and wording, the community possessed a robust collective memory. While such discrepancies appear to have been rare, the structure of the verification process was designed to resolve them definitively.

10.5.4 Ordering the Surahs

The Prophet had guided the placement of verses within their respective surahs during his lifetime, but the surahs themselves also had a specific sequence. Although not strictly chronological, there was a recognized order that the Prophet often used during recitation and in daily prayers. Zayd's team followed that established order, placing the surahs in the arrangement that companions had frequently heard from the Prophet—beginning with Al-Fatihah, followed by Al-Baqarah, and so forth.

10.6 Practical Challenges and Solutions

10.6.1 Collecting Dispersed Materials

Zayd's team likely faced logistical issues. Some companions lived on the outskirts of Medina or had traveled to garrison towns for the Ridda campaigns. Summoning them required time and coordination. Moreover, many written fragments were in personal collections, from palm-stalks to bones, parchment, or papyrus. Handling and organizing these varied materials demanded patience and care.

10.6.2 Ensuring Broad Community Involvement

To ensure trust in the final collection, the compilation process was conducted transparently. People knew of the process and could witness or participate in verifying verses. This broad-based involvement strengthened communal confidence that no single faction or individual was dictating the text. It also helped the new manuscript gain rapid acceptance once completed.

10.6.3 Balancing Military and Administrative Pressures

While the compilation proceeded, Abu Bakr and Umar continued to manage the aftermath of the Ridda Wars. Soldiers were still out in the field, pacifying rebellious tribes. Administrators in Medina juggled the daily tasks of governance, such as tax collection, dispute resolution, and public welfare. Yet, the priority assigned to preserving the Quran ensured that Zayd and his aides had the necessary resources and cooperation.

10.7 Completion of the First Official Codex

10.7.1 Presentation to Abu Bakr

After painstaking work, Zayd's team compiled the verified verses into a single manuscript—a set of bound sheets or leaves. He presented this collection to Abu Bakr, who carefully reviewed the completed project. Abu Bakr, deeply aware of its historic significance, likely consulted with senior companions to affirm the authenticity of what Zayd had produced.

10.7.2 Storage and Protection

The new compilation was entrusted to Abu Bakr during his caliphate, as he was directly responsible for it. This codex was sometimes referred to as a "Mushaf," a term for a collection of written pages. It was understood that this master copy would serve as the definitive reference if future disputes arose.

10.7.3 Universal Acceptance Among the Companions

Given the methodical approach—requiring multiple witnesses for each verse and broad community involvement—the final manuscript faced no significant opposition. Esteemed memorizers and scribes attested to its accuracy, and local teachers began to adjust their personal notes or memorization if they found any minor discrepancies. The fact that the effort was spearheaded by Abu Bakr and Umar, both deeply respected for their piety and closeness to the Prophet, reinforced communal confidence.

10.8 Significance and Impact

10.8.1 Preservation of the Revelation

This first official collection was a watershed moment in Islamic history. For the first time, there existed a single, universally recognized manuscript containing the entire Quran. While memorization remained the primary mode of engagement with the scripture—especially in daily prayers, teaching, and personal devotion—the Mushaf ensured that future generations had a reliable text to consult if differences of opinion arose.

10.8.2 Foundation for Subsequent Efforts

Abu Bakr's compilation set a precedent. During the reign of the third caliph, Uthman ibn Affan, the need would arise to distribute standardized copies of the Quran to distant provinces. But the success of Uthman's effort rested on the foundation Abu Bakr had laid. Without the first collection, the expansion of the Muslim world might have spurred divergent readings, dialectical variations, and potential conflicts over textual integrity.

10.8.3 Unity in Times of Rapid Expansion

Shortly after Abu Bakr's caliphate, Islamic rule extended beyond the Arabian Peninsula into regions like Syria, Iraq, and Egypt. Soldiers, merchants, and teachers carried the Quran with them. The existence of an agreed-upon reference text helped maintain doctrinal cohesion. Even though many new converts would rely on local teachers and memorizers, the knowledge that a master codex existed in the capital city preserved unity around a single version of the revelation.

10.9 Later Custodianship of the Codex

10.9.1 From Abu Bakr to Umar

Abu Bakr served as caliph for about two years, passing away in 634 CE. In his will, he named Umar as his successor. The Mushaf compiled under Abu Bakr's supervision remained in the care of the caliph's office, but practical guardianship might have shifted to Umar himself or to designated scribes. Although details are sparse, historical accounts suggest that Umar and other senior companions kept the codex secure.

10.9.2 Umar's Stewardship and Access

Umar maintained a strong administrative structure in Medina, with continued expansions into Persia, the Levant, and parts of North Africa. While local communities mostly relied on memory and partial written copies, the official Mushaf was the ultimate reference. If any dispute arose over a verse or reading, teachers or scribes could visit Medina to compare their memorized or written text with the central codex.

10.9.3 Safekeeping in Hafsah's Custody

After Umar's assassination in 644 CE, his daughter Hafsah—one of the Prophet's widows—reportedly received custody of the codex. She preserved it meticulously, understanding its gravity. During Uthman's caliphate, when the need for standardized copies arose, Hafsah's codex played a crucial role as the source text. This underscores how the first official manuscript outlived multiple caliphs and became a cornerstone of Islamic scholarship.

Chapter Eleven: Caliph Umar's Period and Continued Expansion

11.1 Introduction

With the passing of Caliph Abu Bakr in 634 CE, Umar ibn al-Khattab assumed the caliphate—an event that would reshape the nascent Muslim state for decades to come. While Abu Bakr's leadership stabilized Arabia after the Prophet Muhammad's death and oversaw the first compilation of the Quran, Umar's rule is often remembered for large-scale military expansions and strong administrative reforms. These developments had a significant impact on the spread of Islam—and, by extension, the dissemination of the Quran—across vast new territories.

In this chapter, we explore Umar's early life and ascent to leadership, his approach to governance and legal matters, and the massive conquests that brought regions like Syria, Egypt, and parts of the Sasanian Empire under Muslim rule. We also examine how this rapid expansion influenced the preservation of the Quranic text. Despite the varied languages and cultures within the expanding empire, the Quran remained a central unifying force. We will see how Umar's leadership reinforced the importance of a standardized text, building upon the compilation completed under Abu Bakr.

11.2 Umar ibn al-Khattab's Background

11.2.1 Early Life and Conversion

Umar was born into the Banu Adi clan of the Quraysh tribe in Mecca, likely around 584 CE. Before converting to Islam, he was known for his strong personality, physical strength, and deep attachment to Meccan traditions. Initially, he opposed the Prophet Muhammad's monotheistic message, worried it would fracture the Quraysh's social fabric and religious customs. However, in a famed story, he set out with the intention of confronting (and possibly harming) Muhammad but instead encountered verses of the Quran that moved him profoundly. Astonished by the text's depth, he embraced Islam, becoming one of its strongest supporters.

11.2.2 Service Under Prophet Muhammad and Abu Bakr

After converting, Umar became a close companion of the Prophet, recognized for his courage in battles and his keen administrative mind. He played a prominent role during the Hijrah to Medina, participated in major military engagements such as the battles of Badr and Uhud, and advised the Prophet on community matters. With the Prophet's passing in 632 CE, Umar supported Abu Bakr's nomination as the first caliph, defending the idea that Muslims required a clear successor to prevent internal chaos.

During Abu Bakr's caliphate (632–634 CE), Umar continued as a top advisor, particularly involved in pacifying rebellious tribes during the Ridda Wars. He was the one who persistently urged Abu Bakr to compile the Quran into a single manuscript to safeguard it against potential losses of memorizers on the battlefield. When Abu Bakr's health deteriorated, he appointed Umar as his successor. Umar's rule began in 634 CE and lasted until his assassination in 644 CE.

11.3 Umar's Character and Leadership Principles

11.3.1 Justice and Accountability

Umar was renowned for his unwavering sense of justice. Stories abound of him walking the streets of Medina at night, observing conditions firsthand to ensure the well-being of the people. He set an example by living modestly, refusing privileges beyond basic needs, and consistently emphasizing accountability. He once declared: "If a mule were to stumble on the road in Iraq, I would fear that God would ask me why I did not maintain the roads for it." This attitude underscored the depth of his moral responsibility.

11.3.2 Simplicity and Humility

Despite ruling an empire that was rapidly expanding to encompass vast regions, Umar's lifestyle remained simple. He continued to wear plain clothing, slept on a simple bed of palm leaves, and had few personal possessions. Even foreign envoys were surprised by his austere living conditions, finding him approachable and free from pomp. This simplicity impressed both Muslims and non-Muslims, reinforcing Islam's message of social equality and responsible governance.

11.3.3 Consultative Governance

While Umar wielded strong authority, he also instituted councils of advisors (shura) to aid in decision-making. He frequently sought opinions from senior companions on military strategies, administrative appointments, and legal matters. This style of consultative leadership balanced decisive action with communal input, mirroring the Quranic encouragement to consult in matters of importance (Quran 42:38).

11.4 Military Conquests and Expansion

11.4.1 Campaigns in Syria and Palestine

Shortly after becoming caliph, Umar continued the military campaigns begun under Abu Bakr. Khalid ibn al-Walid and other generals led forces against the Byzantine Empire in Syria. Cities like Damascus, Homs, and Jerusalem fell under Muslim control through a combination of pitched battles and negotiated surrenders. The conquest of Jerusalem in 637 CE is particularly famous: Umar personally traveled there to accept the city's surrender, demonstrating religious tolerance by safeguarding Christian holy sites.

11.4.2 Expansion into Egypt

Spurred by the successes in Syria, Umar gave permission for an expedition into Egypt under the command of Amr ibn al-As. The province, nominally controlled by the Byzantine Empire, was rife with internal grievances and welcomed the comparatively lower taxes and relative tolerance promised under Muslim rule. Within a few years, major cities like Babylon (near modern Cairo) and Alexandria were brought into the Muslim domain. These swift victories expanded the caliphate's reach to North Africa.

11.4.3 Conquest of the Sasanian Empire (Persia)

Umar also oversaw decisive campaigns against the weakening Sasanian Empire. Major battles, such as the Battle of Qadisiyyah (636 CE) and the Battle of Nahavand (642 CE), broke Sasanian power. Cities like Ctesiphon (near modern-day Baghdad) fell, and large swaths of Persia, from Mesopotamia to the Iranian heartland, came under Muslim governance. This expansion introduced Islam to a culturally and linguistically distinct population, sparking broad interaction between Arab Muslims and Persian traditions.

11.4.4 Administrative and Strategic Vision

Umar's conquests were not chaotic raids but carefully strategized campaigns aimed at long-term governance. Unlike some earlier Arabian raids, these expansions involved establishing administrative centers (amsar), fortifying key cities, and instituting diwan (registers) to distribute stipends to soldiers and their families. The empire's growth under Umar was thus more than territorial; it represented the birth of structured governance that would profoundly influence how the Quran was introduced and taught to diverse populations.

11.5 Impact of Expansion on the Quran's Dissemination

11.5.1 Diverse Languages and Cultures

As the Muslim armies conquered territories inhabited by Aramaic, Coptic, Greek, and Persian speakers, the Quran—primarily in Arabic—encountered new cultural frontiers. Some new converts sought to learn Arabic to fully appreciate the scripture, while others relied on local teachers for explanations in their native tongues. Although the Arabic text remained the official reference, translations of Quranic meanings began informally spreading through teachings and commentaries, allowing non-Arabic speakers to grasp its essential messages.

11.5.2 Need for Qualified Reciters and Teachers

To serve the rapidly growing Islamic population, Umar encouraged knowledgeable companions, memorizers, and scribes to settle in newly conquered regions. These individuals taught the fundamentals of faith, led prayers, and instructed people in Quranic recitation. Cities like Kufa and Basra in Iraq became new centers of Islamic scholarship, attracting companions who established schools of Quranic reading and interpretation. The diaspora of reciters helped maintain fidelity to the standard text, building upon the official compilation from Abu Bakr's era.

11.5.3 Ensuring a Single, Uniform Text

Even though Abu Bakr's compiled Mushaf resided in Medina, the expansions raised questions of textual consistency. While the companions who traveled shared the same memorized text, some minor variations in pronunciation and recitation styles (qira'at) emerged due to linguistic diversity. Umar recognized this potential challenge and supported the principle of referencing the central codex in Medina whenever uncertainty arose. This approach foreshadowed the more formal canonization that would occur under Caliph Uthman.

11.6 Administrative Reforms Under Umar

11.6.1 Formation of Key Administrative Centers

Umar's governance style promoted stability and facilitated the study of the Quran by establishing garrison towns or amsar. Basra (founded 638 CE) and Kufa (founded 638 CE) became hubs where Muslim troops settled with their families, forming self-contained communities. These settlements featured mosques, administrative buildings, and markets, often with an attached dar al-qurra (house of reciters) where the Quran was taught. The presence of skilled companions in these towns greatly advanced Quranic scholarship.

11.6.2 Legal and Social Guidelines

While the Quran served as the primary source of law, Umar also enacted administrative policies inspired by it. For instance, he regulated the land tenure system in newly conquered areas, ensuring local farmers were not dispossessed en masse. Land taxes (kharaj) were set, reflecting both the Prophet's teachings on fairness and the pragmatic need to maintain agricultural productivity. Local populations often contrasted these policies favorably with the oppressive taxes they had experienced under Byzantine or Sasanian rule.

11.6.3 Literacy and Records

One of Umar's notable reforms was improving record-keeping (diwan). Though the primary impetus was tracking soldier stipends and revenues, it also spurred a heightened interest in literacy. Soldiers, administrators, and local officials found themselves in frequent contact with Arabic script. This indirectly supported the proliferation of Quranic texts and commentary, as the same scribes who managed diwan might also engage in writing or copying passages of scripture.

11.7 Relationship with Non-Muslim Populations

11.7.1 The Dhimmi System

With conquests came the responsibility of governing non-Muslim subjects, particularly Christians, Jews, and Zoroastrians. Umar upheld and formalized treaties that allowed these groups to retain their faith, churches, synagogues, and fire temples, provided they paid the jizya (poll tax) and recognized Muslim governance. In many territories, the transition from Byzantine or Sasanian rule to Muslim rule was reportedly smoother than expected, partly because local communities sometimes saw the new rulers as less burdensome.

11.7.2 Influence on Quranic Study

Non-Muslims under Muslim rule became exposed to the Quran's teachings, occasionally attending public recitations. While most did not convert, some engaged in theological discussions, prompting Muslim scholars to deepen their understanding of the text to effectively clarify Islamic beliefs. This interfaith dialogue inspired a more systematic approach to Quranic exegesis (tafsir) among certain companions, who sought to explain verses addressing earlier scriptures and prophets shared by Judaism and Christianity.

11.7.3 Emergence of Intellectual Hubs

Cities like Damascus, Jerusalem, Fustat (near Cairo), and Kufa blossomed into multicultural hubs. Muslim administrators, local scholars, and visiting merchants mingled. In this environment, the Quran was both a unifying text for Muslims and a point of curious interest for non-Muslims. Over time, this laid the groundwork for advanced Quranic studies, grammar, and lexicography, as scholars needed precise knowledge of the language and context to respond to inquiries from various religious communities.

11.8 Umar's Contributions to Quranic Preservation

11.8.1 Reinforcing Abu Bakr's Compilation

Even though the official codex compiled during Abu Bakr's time remained primarily in Medina, Umar championed its authority. He repeatedly reminded newly appointed governors and regional judges that if disputes arose about the proper recitation or wording of the Quran, they should refer back to the central collection. This underscored the importance of a standardized text and curbed the possibility of divergent manuscripts taking root in far-off provinces.

11.8.2 Emphasis on Memorization and Recitation

Umar himself was known to be a Hafiz (memorizer) of the Quran. He often led prayers in the mosque of Medina, reciting long passages in the Fajr (dawn) prayer. His personal devotion to the text exemplified how leaders and common believers alike upheld the practice of memorization. In the newly conquered lands, he encouraged establishing mosques and appointing teachers to instruct fresh converts. This not only expanded the faith but also preserved the text through continuous recitation cycles.

11.8.3 Settling Disputes Over Dialects

In Arabia, Arabic had multiple dialects (lahajat). During the Prophet's lifetime, certain verses could be recited in slightly varied dialectical forms, a concession made for tribes whose pronunciation differed. However, as Islam spread beyond the Peninsula, the risk of confusion or corruption of the text rose. Umar endorsed the principle of reading the Quran in the Qurayshi dialect (the dialect of Mecca and the Prophet) for official and instructional purposes. This move would later gain further impetus under Uthman.

11.9 The Final Years of Umar's Caliphate

11.9.1 Economic and Social Reforms

Umar's last years saw continued military campaigns in Persia and North Africa, but he also devoted attention to internal reforms. He introduced welfare measures, regulated the marketplace, and built canals and roads to facilitate trade. These infrastructural improvements allowed for smoother travel, which in turn helped Islamic scholars move freely between regions, spreading Quranic knowledge.

11.9.2 Assassination and Aftermath

In 644 CE, while leading the morning prayer at the mosque in Medina, Umar was attacked and fatally wounded by a Persian slave named Abu Lu'lu'ah. Umar's impending death thrust the community into mourning. Before dying, Umar appointed a six-member council (shura) to select the next caliph. This council eventually chose Uthman ibn Affan, one of the Prophet's closest companions, who would continue the tradition of consultative leadership.

11.9.3 Legacy for the Quran

When Umar passed away, the Islamic empire stretched from Libya in the west to the edges of Persia in the east. Arabic was becoming a language of administration and religion across these lands. Under Umar's guidance, the authority of Abu Bakr's compiled Mushaf was firmly established. His emphasis on referencing the original codex in Medina and encouraging consistent recitation traditions set the stage for the next major development in Quranic history: the standardization project under Uthman.

Chapter Twelve: Caliph Uthman's Canonization and Distribution of Copies

12.1 Introduction

When Uthman ibn Affan became the third caliph in 644 CE, he inherited an empire that was already vast and still expanding. Under Abu Bakr, the first official codex of the Quran had been compiled, while under Umar, the text was preserved and universally recognized. Yet, as Arabic-speaking armies ventured deeper into foreign lands, linguistic variations in Quranic recitation began surfacing. People from different regions or tribes, newly converted or taught by different companions, sometimes argued over the "correct" pronunciation or reading.

This chapter delves into how Caliph Uthman addressed these emerging discrepancies by creating a standardized version of the Quran. We will explore the motivations behind this decision, the careful steps Uthman took to ensure consistency, and the influential role of scribes like Zayd ibn Thabit. Furthermore, we will examine the distribution of these standardized copies to key Islamic centers and how Uthman's measures shaped the text's transmission. This "canonization" effort remains crucial to the Quran's unbroken authenticity and uniformity to this day.

12.2 Uthman ibn Affan: Background and Leadership

12.2.1 Early Life and Conversion

Uthman was a wealthy and respected member of the Quraysh tribe, known for his gentleness, generosity, and piety. Among the earliest converts to Islam, he married two daughters of the Prophet—first Ruqayyah, and after her passing, Umm Kulthum. Hence, he is sometimes referred to as "Dhun-Nurayn" (the possessor of two lights). Uthman was noted for his financial support of the Muslim community; he once funded an entire military expedition when resources were scarce.

12.2.2 Service Under Abu Bakr and Umar

Like many of the Prophet's close companions, Uthman served diligently under the first two caliphs. He was a trusted advisor to Abu Bakr, contributing resources and counsel during the Ridda Wars. Under Umar, he provided advice on financial and administrative matters, leveraging his mercantile experience. Despite being reserved by nature, Uthman's reputation for honesty and devotion made him a natural candidate for leadership when Umar's council convened to choose the next caliph.

12.2.3 Accession to the Caliphate

Selected by Umar's appointed shura (council) after a period of deliberation, Uthman became caliph in 644 CE. His tenure lasted until 656 CE, a period marked by further territorial expansion but also growing internal tensions. During the early part of his rule, he enjoyed broad acceptance and took on the responsibility of addressing the Quranic recitation issues that had started to arise across the empire.

12.3 Reasons for Standardizing the Quran Under Uthman

12.3.1 Expansion Beyond the Arabian Peninsula

Under Umar, Muslim armies had already marched into Syria, Egypt, and parts of Persia. Uthman's era saw the conquests push further into North Africa, Armenia, and Central Asia. New converts in these distant lands often learned Islam from soldiers or local teachers, each possibly reciting the Quran in slightly different ways. These differences were not necessarily contradictory, but the risk of confusion or argument increased as the empire became more diverse.

12.3.2 Linguistic Variation and Dialectal Readings

During the Prophet's lifetime, some companions recited the Quran in their tribal dialects. The Prophet allowed certain dialectical concessions to make recitation easier for new believers. However, after the Prophet's death, people outside Arabia, or from lesser-known tribes, sometimes insisted that the version they learned was correct. Minor variances in pronunciation could grow into heated disputes. Prominent generals, like Hudhayfah ibn al-Yaman (who served in the campaigns in Armenia and Azerbaijan), reportedly encountered soldiers quarreling over the right "version" of the Quran, prompting him to raise alarms with Uthman.

12.3.3 Preserving Unity

The fear was that if disputes over the Quran's reading escalated, they could harm the sense of unity crucial for a large, multi-ethnic empire. The Quran was not merely a religious text but a unifying constitution. Maintaining a single, definitive standard for the scripture was seen as vital to preventing sectarian splits or the emergence of regional "versions" of Islam.

12.4 Initial Steps: Consultation and Planning

12.4.1 Advice from Hudhayfah ibn al-Yaman

After witnessing the disputes among troops in the Caucasus region, Hudhayfah traveled to Medina and urged Uthman to intervene. He warned that if immediate action was not taken, the community might fragment over variations in recitation. Uthman was deeply concerned. He recognized that a purely oral tradition—even one as robust as in the Arabian culture—was vulnerable to small but cumulative shifts in pronunciation among non-native Arabic speakers.

12.4.2 Council of Senior Companions

Before taking any formal steps, Uthman consulted with leading companions, including Ali ibn Abi Talib, Zubayr ibn al-Awwam, Sa'd ibn Abi Waqqas, and others. Collectively, they agreed that preserving the uniform recitation instituted by the Prophet was imperative. They concurred that the codex originally compiled under Abu Bakr (and guarded by Umar, then Hafsah) should serve as the master reference.

12.4.3 Retrieval of Hafsah's Codex

Hafsah bint Umar, one of the Prophet's widows, had been entrusted with the master codex (the Mushaf) that Abu Bakr and Zayd ibn Thabit had compiled. Uthman requested Hafsah's permission to use this manuscript as the basis for creating official copies. After being assured the original would be returned, she agreed. This moment was pivotal: it ensured that Uthman's standardization would not introduce any textual novelty but would adhere strictly to the earliest compiled version.

12.5 Assembling the Committee for Canonization

12.5.1 Reappointment of Zayd ibn Thabit

Uthman once again enlisted the expertise of Zayd ibn Thabit—who led the initial compilation under Abu Bakr—to head this new project. Zayd's credentials remained impeccable: he was a trusted scribe, a Hafiz, and intimately familiar with the ordering of verses. His direct experience with the first compilation made him an invaluable leader for the second initiative.

12.5.2 Other Scribes and Scholars

Joining Zayd on the committee were several companions from the Quraysh, including Abdullah ibn Zubayr, Sa'id ibn al-As, and Abdur-Rahman ibn al-Harith ibn Hisham. All were known for their deep understanding of Arabic linguistics and the Quranic text. Uthman instructed them: if they encountered any minor differences in dialect or wording, they should rely on the Qurayshi dialect—the Prophet's dialect—for the final standard. This principle reflected a tradition that the Quran was originally revealed in the tongue of Quraysh, thereby securing textual uniformity.

12.5.3 Verification Against the Master Copy

The committee used Hafsah's codex as their baseline, checking each verse carefully. Whenever they found any variant reading in regional manuscripts, they prioritized the original compilation's text. This method ensured continuity with the earlier compilation, preventing any suspicion of alteration. As with Abu Bakr's project, public oversight and the involvement of recognized authorities helped maintain communal trust in the outcome.

12.6 Methodology of Creating Standard Copies

12.6.1 Recitation and Comparison

Committee members recited verses from memory, comparing them with the text of Hafsah's codex. If differences emerged in slight wording or dialectical variations, the committee decided in favor of the form found in the master copy or, in unclear cases, the Qurayshi dialect. This approach not only resolved disputes but also standardized the script.

12.6.2 Scripting and Spelling Norms

Writing in Arabic script during the mid-7th century differed from modern conventions. Vowel markings, diacritical points for letters like "b," "t," or "th," and other punctuation did not exist in the form we know today. Nevertheless, the scribes strove for clarity, employing the recognized script forms of the time. It was understood that proficient readers—especially those who memorized the Quran—could discern the correct pronunciation from the context, even without modern diacritical marks.

12.6.3 Final Review

Once the new copies were drafted, they underwent a thorough review. Uthman, the committee members, and other memorizers recited passages to cross-check. The objective was to ensure absolute fidelity to the Mushaf compiled under Abu Bakr and subsequently validated over the years. Once consensus was reached that the text matched the recognized standard, the final versions were ready for dissemination.

12.7 Distribution to Major Islamic Centers

12.7.1 Sending Copies to Key Cities

Uthman is reported to have prepared several official copies of this standardized text—commonly referred to as the "Uthmanic codices"—and sent them to major administrative centers of the Islamic empire. These cities likely included:

- **Kufa** in Iraq
- **Basra** in Iraq
- **Damascus** in Syria
- **Fustat** (near modern Cairo) in Egypt
- **Mecca** in Arabia

A master copy was kept in Medina, the caliphate's capital. Some accounts mention that additional copies might have been dispatched to Yemen or Bahrain, though documentation on these is less certain.

12.7.2 Appointment of Quranic Teachers

Along with these bound texts, Uthman arranged for skilled reciters—companions or senior students of the companions—to accompany the Mushafs. Their responsibility was to teach the local populations the correct recitation (qira'ah) and ensure that any partial or private manuscripts would be revised to match the official standard. By marrying the written text with living reciters, Uthman ensured that both the script and the oral tradition aligned.

12.7.3 Instruction to Destroy Variants

One controversial step Uthman took was to instruct provincial governors and officials to destroy or burn any unofficial manuscripts that conflicted with the new standardized copies. Though harsh by modern standards, this measure aimed to unify the Muslim community behind a single text and prevent future disputes. Many companions supported this action, viewing it as necessary to eliminate confusion. Critics occasionally objected, but the majority recognized the measure as a unifying step rather than an act of suppressing genuine variation.

12.8 Significance of Uthman's Canonization

12.8.1 Uniformity Across the Empire

Uthman's standardization succeeded in creating a single recognized text that new generations of Muslims could learn. The empire now stretched from North Africa to Central Asia, yet believers from these distant regions recited the same Quranic verses in the same order and wording. This remarkable unity, in an era without modern communication, underscored the deep devotion Muslims held for their scripture.

12.8.2 Preservation of the Oral Tradition

Although a single text was now official, oral memorization did not diminish. On the contrary, the presence of a standardized script, combined with dedicated instructors, reinforced the oral tradition. Quranic schools (kuttab) and study circles continued to emphasize memorization, ensuring that recitation accuracy was continually cross-checked against both the textual copy and the living chain (isnad) of reciters going back to the Prophet.

12.8.3 Minimizing Sectarian Schisms

By standardizing the text, Uthman forestalled potential sectarian rifts rooted in variant recitations. While disagreements over political or theological issues would eventually arise within the Muslim community (as seen in later civil strife), the Quran itself remained a shared reference, largely free from textual fragmentation. This textual unity played a stabilizing role during the tumultuous periods that followed, including the first Muslim civil war (the Fitnah) after Uthman's assassination.

12.9 Controversies and Clarifications

12.9.1 Allegations of Omissions or Changes

Over time, critics—both within and outside the Muslim community—have raised allegations that certain verses were omitted or altered during Uthman's standardization. However, early historical sources and the consensus of companions indicate that no changes were introduced; the Uthmanic codex directly relied on Abu Bakr's original compilation, which had itself gone through rigorous verification. Prominent companions like Ali ibn Abi Talib publicly endorsed Uthman's actions, dispelling rumors of textual tampering.

12.9.2 Different Readings Within Allowed Limits

Even after Uthman's standardization, multiple legitimate recitation methods (qira'at) survived. These were not contradictions in text but variations in pronunciation, vowel lengthening, or slight differences in consonantal reading recognized as valid by the Prophet. Over the centuries, Islamic scholars meticulously documented these recitations, ensuring that each had a reliable chain of transmission. The Uthmanic codex thus remained the foundation, with recognized qira'at existing as authorized variations of reading the same script.

12.9.3 The Issue of "Seven Ahruf"

Islamic tradition references the notion that the Quran was revealed "in seven ahruf" (sometimes translated as "seven modes" or "seven ways"). Debates persist over the exact meaning. Some interpret ahruf as dialectal variations, while others see them as deeper nuances in expression. In any case, Uthman's codification is viewed as having preserved the essential meaning of these modes in a single, authorized text, consistent with the Prophet's original recitations.

12.10 Later Developments in Quranic Codices

12.10.1 Emergence of Diacritical Marks

In Uthman's time, Arabic texts generally lacked diacritical points and vowel signs. Within a few decades, as more non-Arabs embraced Islam, confusion arose over letters that looked similar (e.g., ن, ث, ت, ب, etc.). To assist new learners, scholars introduced dots and marks to clarify pronunciation. By the late Umayyad period, short vowels (fatha, kasra, damma) were being added. These developments were purely orthographic aids and did not alter the consonantal skeleton of the Uthmanic codex.

12.10.2 The Rise of Illumination and Calligraphy

From the time of Uthman's distribution onward, copying the Quran became a sacred craft. Over the centuries, calligraphers developed distinct scripts—Kufic, Naskh, Thuluth, etc.—to produce beautifully illuminated manuscripts. Despite stylistic flourishes, the underlying text consistently traced back to the Uthmanic archetype. This blend of artistry and textual fidelity highlighted the community's reverence for the written word of God.

12.10.3 Preservation Through Generations

Thanks to Uthman's standardization, the text that spread throughout the Muslim world was remarkably uniform. Even surviving early Quranic manuscripts from the first few centuries of Islam—like those discovered in the Great Mosque of Sana'a, or partial fragments found in the Topkapi Palace and other libraries—show minor orthographic or scribal variations but no substantive differences in content. This fidelity contrasts notably with the textual evolution seen in many other ancient writings.

12.11 Uthman's Later Rule and Assassination

12.11.1 Political Challenges and Opposition

Despite Uthman's revered status as a companion and his success in preserving the Quran's unity, his administration encountered growing unrest. Accusations of nepotism, disagreements over provincial appointments, and economic inequalities fueled dissatisfaction. Some critics felt that his distribution of certain governorships to relatives was unjust. Uthman, known for his lenient, gentle nature, sometimes hesitated to remove controversial figures, exacerbating public anger.

12.11.2 Siege and Murder

In 656 CE, protests escalated into a siege of Uthman's house in Medina. Rebels from Egypt and other provinces demanded reforms. Negotiations broke down, and a violent faction entered Uthman's home, assassinating him while he reportedly recited the Quran. His tragic death sparked the first major civil war in Islamic history (the Fitnah), pitting factions led by Ali ibn Abi Talib, Aisha, and Muawiyah against one another.

12.11.3 Legacy for the Quran

Uthman's assassination shook the Muslim community. Nonetheless, the standardized Mushaf he had overseen became the bedrock for all Quranic texts thereafter. The warring parties might have disagreed on political leadership, but they did not dispute the authenticity of the Quranic text. This shared acceptance served as a unifying factor even in a time of deep political strife.

Chapter Thirteen: Caliph Ali's Time and Early Quranic Debates

13.1 Introduction

After the assassination of Caliph Uthman in 656 CE, the Muslim community entered a period of intense political turmoil. Ali ibn Abi Talib, cousin and son-in-law of the Prophet Muhammad, was chosen as the fourth caliph. Although revered for his piety, knowledge, and close kinship with the Prophet, Ali faced significant challenges. Regional factions, grievances about Uthman's governance, and the question of justice for the slain caliph led to unrest and civil wars.

Despite the crisis, the Quran itself continued to serve as the unifying scripture for Muslims of varied allegiances. Yet new debates about interpretation, authority, and recitation practices began to emerge, fueled by political tensions and the empire's cultural diversity. In this chapter, we will examine Ali's caliphate (656–661 CE), with attention to the major conflicts that shaped his reign and the early disputes surrounding the Quran. Although the standard text had been established under Uthman, questions about reading styles and interpretive authority became more pronounced. We will see how Ali's era laid foundations for future theological and exegetical developments, even amidst civil strife.

13.2 Ali ibn Abi Talib: Background and Accession

13.2.1 Early Life and Relationship to the Prophet

Ali was born in Mecca around 600 CE to Abu Talib, the Prophet Muhammad's uncle. He grew up in the same household as the Prophet and accepted Islam as a child, making him one of the earliest believers. From the Hijrah onward, Ali's bravery and devotion stood out: he famously slept in the Prophet's bed the night before the flight to Medina to confuse potential assassins, and he participated in nearly every major battle, such as Badr, Uhud, and Khaybar.

Ali also married Fatimah, the Prophet's daughter, strengthening his familial ties to Muhammad. Admired for his deep knowledge of the Quran and jurisprudence, Ali was often called upon to solve legal issues. The Prophet is reported to have praised Ali's judgment, and many companions sought his advice on complex matters. These qualities contributed to Ali's reputation as a wise scholar of Islam.

13.2.2 Circumstances Leading to His Caliphate

Following Uthman's murder, Medina was gripped by chaos. Demonstrators who had besieged Uthman's home demanded a new leader who would address their grievances—chief among them, justice for Uthman's death and reforms to perceived abuses. Many of these rebels insisted that Ali should become caliph. Although he was initially reluctant, the majority of Medina's prominent figures agreed that Ali was the most qualified candidate, given his closeness to the Prophet and his recognized piety.

Thus, Ali took the caliphate in mid-656 CE, hoping to restore order. However, the circumstances of Uthman's assassination divided the community: some believed that Ali should punish the rebels immediately; others felt the situation required a more deliberative approach. The resulting tensions would overshadow much of Ali's reign.

13.3 Major Conflicts During Ali's Caliphate

13.3.1 The Battle of the Camel

One of the earliest flashpoints was the uprising led by A'ishah, the Prophet's widow, alongside notable companions like Talhah and Zubayr. They sought immediate retribution against the killers of Uthman. Ali attempted to negotiate, but misunderstandings and provocations escalated into armed conflict near Basra in late 656 CE. Known as the Battle of the Camel (due to A'ishah riding a camel on the battlefield), the confrontation ended in Ali's victory. However, the loss of many companions on both sides deepened rifts within the ummah.

13.3.2 Confrontation with Muawiyah

Another major source of opposition was Muawiyah ibn Abi Sufyan, the governor of Syria and a relative of Uthman. Holding Ali responsible—or at least negligent—in pursuing Uthman's murderers, Muawiyah refused to recognize Ali's authority. Tensions culminated in the Battle of Siffin (657 CE) along the Euphrates River. The conflict nearly ended in decisive combat, but it was halted by arbitration when soldiers on Muawiyah's side raised copies of the Quran on spears, calling for the Book of God to judge their dispute.

13.3.3 Emergence of the Kharijites

The arbitration process following Siffin displeased a faction within Ali's own supporters, who believed that "judgment belongs only to God" and opposed human arbitration as a betrayal of Quranic principles. This group broke away, becoming known as the "Kharijites" (from kharaja, "to leave"). They condemned both Ali and Muawiyah for accepting arbitration, arguing the Quran should have been the sole judge. The Kharijites would become a significant force, challenging Ali militarily at Nahrawan and contributing to the strife that permeated his reign.

13.4 Quranic Appeals in Political Disputes

13.4.1 The Quran Raised on Spears

During the Battle of Siffin, Muawiyah's forces famously placed Quranic manuscripts on spear tips to demand an end to the fighting and arbitration using the scripture. This tactic leveraged the high reverence Muslims held for the Quran. Ali's troops were divided on how to respond: many refused to fight once the Quran was invoked, while others believed it was a political ploy. Ultimately, Ali accepted arbitration to avoid the stigma of fighting against the symbol of the Quran, but this concession alienated a portion of his followers.

13.4.2 Citing Verses for Justification

All sides in the political conflicts of this era used Quranic verses to justify their stances. For example, those who opposed Ali cited verses about justice and retribution, claiming that he had failed to punish Uthman's killers. Ali's side responded with verses highlighting obedience to rightful leadership and the dangers of rebellion. The disagreements were often less about the text itself and more about interpreting and applying it to complex political realities. However, the frequency of scriptural references underscored the Quran's central role as the communal arbiter of values.

13.4.3 Early Seeds of Exegesis Disputes

These events laid early groundwork for interpretive debates. As different factions claimed Quranic support for their positions, questions arose about who had the legitimate authority to interpret scripture. Should it be the caliph, recognized scholars, or any believer guided by the text's literal meaning? Such tensions did not lead to open challenges of the Quranic text—Uthman's codification remained authoritative—but they did spur deeper theological inquiries that would blossom in later generations.

13.5 Ali's Relationship to the Quran

13.5.1 Reputation for Quranic Knowledge

Ali was widely acknowledged as one of the most knowledgeable companions regarding the Quran. The Prophet Muhammad is said to have prayed that God would guide Ali's tongue and heart in the Book's understanding. Ali's sermons, letters, and rulings, some of which appear in collections like Nahj al-Balagha (compiled centuries later), exhibit a deep familiarity with Quranic themes and Arabic eloquence. He often drew upon the text to articulate principles of justice, piety, and governance.

13.5.2 Promoting Recitation and Study

Throughout his caliphate, Ali continued the tradition of encouraging memorization and correct recitation. He appointed qualified reciters to lead prayers in regional capitals, and he admonished judges to ground their decisions in Quranic norms. In Kufa—Ali's seat of government after moving from Medina—he fostered circles of scholars who taught the Quran and transmitted hadith. This emphasis ensured that even amidst civil disorder, the impetus to preserve and propagate the scripture did not fade.

13.5.3 Views on Interpretation

Although Ali did not produce a formal written tafsir (exegesis), his recorded teachings suggest a balanced approach. He stressed the necessity of understanding the Quran's broader context, urging believers not to isolate verses out of context or manipulate them for personal agendas. He denounced literalist readings that ignored the holistic message of justice and compassion, and he also cautioned against overly allegorical interpretations that stripped verses of their clear meaning. His perspective hinted at a middle path, foreshadowing later Sunni and Shi'a exegetical traditions in which Ali is revered as an authoritative source.

13.6 The Kharijites and Their Quranic Rhetoric

13.6.1 Origins and Ideology

The Kharijites' break from Ali was rooted in their strict reading of verses emphasizing God's supreme judgment. They argued that human arbitration compromised God's exclusive authority. Declaring both Ali and Muawiyah to be sinners, they insisted that leadership should be based on piety alone, not lineage or past achievements. They scorned any form of compromise that, in their eyes, diluted the Quran's clear moral imperatives.

13.6.2 Quranic Literalism

Kharijite communities, spread across southern Iraq and Arabia, adopted a literalist view of the Quran. They invoked passages underscoring the equality of believers and the necessity of immediate justice against wrongdoing. This stance led to harsh treatment of those they perceived as sinners, including acts of violence against travelers or local officials who would not denounce Ali and Muawiyah. Their approach demonstrated how political fragmentation could trigger extreme readings of the scripture.

13.6.3 Impact on Future Debates

Though a minority, the Kharijites set a precedent for later Islamic movements that would appeal to strict, unyielding interpretations of the Quran to critique mainstream leadership. Their stance triggered responses from more moderate theologians, who defended the principle that the Quran must be interpreted with awareness of context and Prophetic tradition. While Kharijism gradually diminished as a major political force, small Kharijite communities survived in parts of North Africa and Oman, carrying on distinct recitational and doctrinal practices.

13.7 Early Developments in Quranic Interpretation

13.7.1 The Necessity of Context (Asbab al-Nuzul)

Amid the controversies of Ali's caliphate, companions increasingly referred to the circumstances of revelation (asbab al-nuzul) to clarify why certain verses were revealed and how they should be applied. For instance, verses revealed in wartime were distinguished from those addressing peacetime ethics, preventing misapplication. Ali himself encouraged such distinctions, instructing believers to recall the historical background of a verse before wielding it in arguments.

13.7.2 Growth of Oral Tafsir Traditions

During Ali's rule, no major written tafsir was compiled, but oral explanations of verses spread widely. Students of prominent companions (like Ibn Abbas, Ibn Mas'ud, and Ubayy ibn Ka'b) collected interpretive statements that shed light on ambiguous passages. This emergent oral tradition laid the basis for future exegetical writings. Although Ali's reign was short, the intensity of political-religious disputes stimulated deeper engagement with the text's meaning.

13.7.3 Influence of Ali's Teachings

Ali's speeches, especially in Kufa, contained numerous Quranic references that future generations would analyze. He illustrated how to derive moral lessons from narratives about past prophets and insisted on reading the Quran as a complete guide for both personal piety and social justice. While immediate commentators did not produce a cohesive "Ali tafsir," they incorporated his quotations into the evolving scholarship of Quranic explanation.

13.8 Preservation and Use of Uthman's Mushaf During Ali's Reign

13.8.1 Continued Validation of the Standard Text

Despite political upheavals, the text standardized by Uthman remained undisputed in content. Ali, who had initially been among those who recognized Uthman's codex, never challenged its authority. Even when factions fought bitterly over governance, none advocated discarding the official Mushaf. This broad consensus attested to the thorough acceptance of the Uthmanic text as the final repository of revelation.

13.8.2 Copies in Key Cities

Regional centers like Kufa and Basra, where Ali's support was strong, had Uthmanic Mushafs. Reciters taught from these copies, ensuring that local memorization aligned with the standard. The same was true in Damascus, where Muawiyah held sway. Although Muawiyah and Ali were political adversaries, both adhered to the same Quranic text. Thus, ironically, the scripture remained a point of unity even as leadership struggles raged.

13.8.3 No Revision or Alteration

No evidence suggests any attempt to revise or alter the Uthmanic text during Ali's caliphate. Indeed, the widespread conflicts made it impractical to undertake new codification efforts. More importantly, the community viewed the Mushaf as sacrosanct, and its textual integrity was beyond dispute. The era's anxieties centered on correct interpretation and application rather than rewriting or reordering verses.

13.9 Ali's Assassination and Aftermath

13.9.1 Murder in Kufa

In 661 CE, during the early morning hours, while Ali led prayers at the Great Mosque of Kufa, a Kharijite named Ibn Muljam attacked him with a poisoned sword. Ali succumbed to his wounds two days later, leaving his followers in disarray. His assassination—like that of Uthman—marked the second time a caliph was violently removed from office, underscoring the gravity of the internal conflicts.

13.9.2 Succession by Hasan and Muawiyah's Rise

Ali's eldest son, Hasan, briefly succeeded him. However, under pressure from Muawiyah's forces and to prevent further bloodshed, Hasan abdicated and recognized Muawiyah as caliph. This move ended the civil war for a time and initiated the Umayyad dynasty (661–750 CE). Ali's supporters, who later became known as Shi'at Ali (the party of Ali), continued to revere his family lineage. The seeds of the Sunni-Shi'a divide trace back, in large part, to these events.

13.9.3 Legacy for the Quran

While Ali's death signaled the end of the Rashidun (Rightly Guided) Caliphs period, the foundation for Quranic scholarship was already strong. Despite political divides, the standard text survived unaltered. The interpretive debates sparked under Ali's rule informed later theological discussions, including how to handle complex verses about governance, obedience, and rebellion. Ali himself remained a symbol of Quranic knowledge and piety for Muslims across sectarian lines.

13.10 Early Theological and Legal Debates Concerning the Quran

13.10.1 The Role of Reason in Interpretation

A hallmark of the disputes in Ali's era was the question of whether believers could apply personal judgment (ra'y) in interpreting the Quran or if they should rely solely on the literal text and the Prophet's traditions. The Kharijites tended toward literalism, while others accepted reasoned analogy (qiyas) under the guidance of recognized scholars. Although these debates did not yield formal "schools" of law and theology just yet, they provided the impetus for the jurisprudential structures that would flourish in the Umayyad and Abbasid periods.

13.10.2 Differentiation from Hadith

As companions passed away, the difference between the Quran and Prophetic traditions (hadith) became more clearly delineated. The Quran was the unchanged word of God, whereas hadith were narrations about the Prophet's sayings and actions. Ali's emphasis on the Prophet's example—alongside the Quran—reinforced the practice of cross-referencing hadith to clarify ambiguous verses. However, no comprehensive hadith collections existed yet; such compilations would come in the 2nd and 3rd centuries AH.

13.10.3 Early Seeds of Rationalist vs. Traditionalist Views

Some circles in Iraq, influenced by Greek thought and local intellectual traditions, began applying rational methods to interpret certain theological aspects of the Quran (for instance, about divine attributes or free will). Traditionalists insisted that believers accept the text without delving into speculative explanations. Although these divides were not deeply institutionalized during Ali's lifetime, they foreshadowed the Mutazilite and Ash'arite controversies of later centuries.

13.11 Long-Term Influence of Ali's Era on Quranic Studies

13.11.1 Quranic Memorization and Teaching Tradition

Ali's move to Kufa made the city a center for Quranic scholarship. Students from across the empire traveled there to study. The recitational traditions that developed in Kufa (often associated with companions like Ibn Mas'ud) took root, giving rise to recognized qira'at lines. Over the next century, these recitation schools would systematically record the chain of transmitters, ensuring accurate preservation of the standard text.

13.11.2 Inspiring Tafsir Literature

Ali's statements and sermons, some citing the historical circumstances of specific verses, influenced the earliest generation of mufassirun (Quranic exegetes). They quoted Ali's insights on moral and spiritual themes, highlighting his reputation for melding the Quran with rational and ethical reflection. Even though he left no official tafsir, the memory of his teachings circulated, forming part of the bedrock for classical exegesis.

13.11.3 Shi'a Perspectives on the Quran

For those who later identified with Ali's lineage (Shi'a Muslims), the fourth caliph's stance carried unique authority. While they accepted the Uthmanic codex in textual form—rejecting allegations that it was missing certain verses—they often cited Ali's interpretive authority as second only to the Prophet. Over time, Shi'a scholarship placed particular emphasis on verses referencing the Prophet's family (Ahl al-Bayt), seeing Ali's presence in such passages as central to proper interpretation. However, on the fundamental matter of the Quran's text, mainstream Shi'a views aligned with the standard Mushaf.

Chapter Fourteen: Quranic Manuscripts and Early Arabic Scripts

14.1 Introduction

From the Prophet Muhammad's lifetime through the caliphates of Abu Bakr, Umar, Uthman, and Ali, the Quran was preserved primarily through a combination of memorization and simple written materials. Once Uthman's standardization had taken place, official copies of the Mushaf spread to major regions of the rapidly expanding Muslim world. As the Islamic empire matured—especially under the Umayyad and later Abbasid dynasties—efforts to refine Arabic writing systems and produce more sophisticated manuscripts flourished.

In this chapter, we explore the physical evolution of Quranic manuscripts from humble parchments to more elaborate codices. We delve into the development of early Arabic scripts, the introduction of diacritical marks and vowels to aid non-Arabic speakers, and the influence of regional art and calligraphy. Even though the text remained the same, how it was written, decorated, and standardized underwent significant changes. These shifts not only reveal a growing reverence for the written word of God but also demonstrate how Muslim scribes adapted to the empire's linguistic diversity and cultural exchanges.

14.2 Early Writing Materials and Methods

14.2.1 Parchment and Papyrus

During the first century after the Hijrah, the main materials for writing in the Middle East included parchment (made from animal skins) and papyrus (imported from Egypt). Parchment was durable but relatively expensive, while papyrus was cheaper yet less long-lasting. The official Mushafs sent by Uthman were likely written on parchment because of its durability and prestige. Most small, personal copies—if they existed—might have been on papyrus scrolls or smaller parchment leaves. Over time, as the Muslim empire grew, the supply of papyrus improved, especially in Egyptian territories.

14.2.2 Leather, Bones, and Palm Stalks in Earlier Eras

During the Prophet's time and the immediate decades afterward, some verses of the Quran had been recorded on whatever materials were available: leather scraps, camel shoulder blades, or flattened palm stalks. By the Umayyad period (661–750 CE), however, the practice of writing entire Mushafs on such rudimentary surfaces diminished in favor of more standardized codices on parchment or papyrus. Still, these earlier materials played a crucial role in the initial preservation efforts before the Uthmanic standard became widespread.

14.2.3 Emergence of the Codex Format

Although scrolls were common in the ancient Near East, the codex format (separate pages bound together) gained popularity among Muslims, partly influenced by interactions with Byzantine practices. The codex allowed easier navigation between surahs and verses. By the late Umayyad period, many Qurans were produced as codices, making reading and reference more convenient. This shift accelerated the development of standardized page layouts and writing styles.

14.3 Early Arabic Scripts: Kufic and Beyond

14.3.1 The Nature of Pre-Islamic Arabic Script

Before Islam, Arabic script had evolved from Nabatean and other Semitic alphabets. It was typically written without diacritical dots (to differentiate letters like ث , ت , ب) or short vowels (the fatha, damma, and kasra). People who spoke Arabic natively could usually parse the intended meaning from context. However, for new converts—and especially non-Arabs—this lack of markers made reading difficult.

14.3.2 Development of the Kufic Script

Named after the Iraqi city of Kufa, Kufic script became one of the earliest distinctive styles for writing the Quran. It was characterized by:

- **Angular, blocky shapes**: Letters were composed of straight lines and bold angles rather than curves.
- **Horizontal layout**: Words were often spaced out in a way that gave the text a stately appearance.
- **Lack of vowel markings**: Early Kufic manuscripts typically had no signs to indicate short vowels, reflecting the original practice.

Kufic was considered suitable for major inscriptions and official manuscripts due to its clarity and solemn aesthetic. Although some variations existed—like the more elongated Mashq style—Kufic served as the hallmark of early monumental Quranic writing.

14.3.3 Hijazi Scripts

Parallel to Kufic, certain scripts used in Mecca and Medina are collectively referred to as Hijazi scripts. These were often more slanted, with a faster, more casual style suited for everyday writing. In the earliest centuries, Mushafs might incorporate both Hijazi and Kufic elements, though over time, scribes increasingly preferred Kufic for formal Quranic manuscripts, especially those destined for mosques or official distribution.

14.4 The Introduction of Diacritical Marks

14.4.1 The Challenge for Non-Arabic Speakers

As Islam spread into non-Arab regions—like Persia, Egypt, and the Levant—many new Muslims struggled to read the Quran in its bare consonantal form. Letters such as ب (b) and ت (t), which look identical without dots, caused confusion. Additionally, short vowels, essential for correct pronunciation, were not indicated in the script. Although memorization and oral transmission helped, a written aid became increasingly necessary.

14.4.2 Early Efforts by Abu al-Aswad al-Du'ali

Tradition credits Abu al-Aswad al-Du'ali (d. 688 CE) with pioneering a system of vowel markings in Basra. Concerned about non-Arab learners mispronouncing the Quran, he placed dots or small marks to indicate short vowels and certain phonetic clues. Though rudimentary compared to modern vowel signs, these initial efforts laid the groundwork for more refined systems.

14.4.3 Expansion Under Umayyad Patronage

During the Umayyad era, governors and scholars pushed for improved notation, especially in major centers like Damascus, Kufa, and Basra. Over time, scribes replaced or supplemented Abu al-Aswad's system of dots with distinct shapes for each vowel sound, eventually introducing symbols for tanwin (the indefinite nasal "-an," "-in," "-un"). They also started marking hamzah (the glottal stop) and shaddah (doubling a consonant). These enhancements aimed to standardize pronunciation for a diverse empire, ensuring the recited text aligned with the inherited tradition from the Prophet's companions.

14.5 Evolution of Scripts and Aesthetics

14.5.1 Transition from Early Kufic to Later Styles

By the 8th and 9th centuries CE, Kufic script itself underwent stylistic changes. Some scribes made it more decorative for prestigious Qurans, elongating horizontal strokes and introducing ornamental flourishes. Simultaneously, cursive scripts—like Naskh—started to appear in less formal writings. Naskh featured more curves and joined letters, eventually becoming a dominant style for everyday use and smaller, more portable Qurans.

14.5.2 Decorative Elements and Illumination

As the Muslim empire stabilized and wealth increased, scribes and artisans began adorning Quranic manuscripts with gold illumination, geometric designs, and vegetal motifs. Inspired by Byzantine and Persian art, these decorations never depicted living beings—reflecting Islamic norms against figurative imagery in religious contexts. Instead, elaborate frames or headings marked surah beginnings. Such embellishments communicated reverence for the text, transforming manuscripts into works of sacred art.

14.5.3 Standard Page Layouts

Over time, scribes agreed upon conventional ways to arrange text on each page. Often, they placed a surah heading in a decorative band, sometimes in gold or colored ink, followed by lines of script with consistent spacing. Marginal markers indicated verse counts or section divisions (rukūʿ). By the Abbasid period, some Mushafs were produced in large sizes for display in mosques, while others were smaller, designed for personal devotion. Uniformity in layout helped readers locate verses and surahs quickly.

14.6 The Role of Royal Patronage

14.6.1 Umayyad Support for Quranic Arts

The Umayyad caliphs (661–750 CE), particularly from their base in Damascus, commissioned impressive mosques—like the Great Mosque of Damascus—and adorned them with Quranic inscriptions. To produce these monumental inscriptions, skilled calligraphers honed large-scale Kufic writing. The Umayyads also donated lavishly bound Mushafs to major cities. Though early Umayyad rule was overshadowed by political controversies, their architectural projects and artistic patronage significantly influenced the growth of Quranic calligraphy.

14.6.2 Abbasid Flourishing in Baghdad

With the Abbasid revolution (750 CE) and the founding of Baghdad, a new cultural hub emerged. Abbasid rulers, positioning themselves as patrons of learning and art, fostered widespread translation movements (e.g., Greek philosophical works into Arabic) and invested in sophisticated calligraphy for the Quran. Scholarly circles in Baghdad refined diacritical systems, producing standard reference copies of the Quran. They also compiled treatises on Arabic grammar and orthography, ensuring scribes had formal guidelines for writing divine text.

14.6.3 Regional Dynasties and Diffusion

As the caliphate fragmented into local dynasties—like the Aghlabids in North Africa, the Umayyads in al-Andalus (Spain), and the Fatimids in Egypt—patronage of Quranic manuscripts continued. Each region developed stylistic variations. For instance, in North Africa and al-Andalus, Maghribi script emerged with unique looping forms. Despite these differences, the underlying consonantal text traced back to the Uthmanic archetype, reaffirming the universal continuity of the Quranic content.

14.7 Evidence from Early Manuscripts

14.7.1 Sana'a Manuscripts

One of the most remarkable findings in modern times is the cache of early Quranic fragments discovered in the Great Mosque of Sana'a, Yemen. Dating to the first two centuries of Islam, these manuscripts exhibit Hijazi and Kufic scripts and confirm the stability of the textual content. While some show slight orthographic variances (e.g., spelling of certain words), no substantive differences in meaning occur. Scholars analyzing these leaves have found them consistent with the Uthmanic standard, underscoring the text's continuity.

14.7.2 Topkapi, Samarkand, and Other Famous Codices

Various libraries and museums around the world possess ancient Quranic manuscripts that tradition sometimes associates with the earliest companions. For instance, the Topkapi Palace Museum in Istanbul claims to hold an Uthmanic manuscript, though modern scholarship suggests it is slightly later, probably from the Umayyad era. The Samarkand Codex, housed in Tashkent, Uzbekistan, similarly exhibits an early Kufic style but with certain design elements that place it post-Uthman. Nonetheless, textual comparison shows they align with the standard Mushaf in content.

14.7.3 Palimpsests and Hidden Texts

In some cases, scribes reused parchment by scraping off older text. Modern technology such as multispectral imaging can reveal these underlying writings—called palimpsests. Even these older layers usually confirm the same consonantal skeleton of the Quran, though occasionally they record minor scribal mistakes or earlier orthographic practices. These findings provide a fascinating window into the scribal processes and reaffirm the essential uniformity of the Quranic text.

14.8 Ongoing Uniformity Amid Script Evolution

14.8.1 Distinction Between Text and Art

Throughout the centuries, the visual presentation of the Quran became increasingly elaborate, but the words themselves—their order and essential letters—remained unchanged. Scribes took great care to avoid altering even the smallest detail of the Uthmanic consonantal structure. If an error slipped in, it was typically corrected or the page was replaced. The distinction between stable textual content and evolving artistic form was a hallmark of Muslim scribal culture.

14.8.2 Oral Transmission as the Final Safeguard

Even as manuscripts became more common, the oral tradition continued to serve as a powerful check. Huffadh (memorizers) recited in mosques and study sessions, detecting any unintentional scribal mistakes. Because the Quran was recited daily in communal prayers—particularly the shorter surahs—people of all social classes had some portion memorized. This wide distribution of knowledge made it exceedingly difficult for any inaccurate copy to gain traction.

14.8.3 Adaptation for Educational Purposes

With growing populations of non-native Arabic speakers, educators adapted manuscripts to include helpful markings. By the 8th and 9th centuries CE, fuller diacritical systems were standard in teaching copies, ensuring novices could pronounce the text accurately. Meanwhile, more experienced readers often used copies with minimal markings, relying on their knowledge to supply vowels. This dual approach allowed the Quran to be accessible to beginners and also elegant in advanced calligraphic renditions.

14.9 The Spread of Multiple Recitation Traditions

14.9.1 Qira'at (Modes of Recitation)

Although the Uthmanic text was uniform in its consonantal form, recognized variants in pronunciation and vocalization—known as qira'at—emerged from the leading companions in cities like Mecca, Medina, Kufa, Basra, and Damascus. These traditions were carefully documented, each with a chain of transmission back to the Prophet's companions. Some differences included elongation of vowels, assimilation of certain letters, or slightly alternate ways to read words with the same spelling.

14.9.2 Canonical and Non-Canonical Readings

By the 3rd and 4th centuries AH, scholars like Abu Bakr ibn Mujahid (d. 324 AH) classified qira'at into categories: the "Seven" (later Ten) canonical readings recognized as wholly valid, and others considered irregular (shadh). Despite this classification, all canonical qira'at adhered to the same basic Uthmanic text. Differences were in vocalization or minor letter shapes, reflecting permissible variation from the Prophet's era.

14.9.3 Tying Recitations to the Written Script

As diacritics and vowels became standard in written Mushafs, scribes often chose a specific qira'ah to represent. For instance, a Mushaf produced in Kufa might reflect the reading transmitted by Hafs from Asim, while one in Medina might follow the reading of Nafi'. In each case, the underlying consonantal skeleton was consistent, but the scribal vowel symbols reflected the local or chosen recitation method. Over time, the Hafs 'an Asim reading (from Kufa) became predominant in many parts of the world.

14.10 Scholarly Institutions and Manuscript Production

14.10.1 Emergence of Libraries

As Islamic governance stabilized, major cities like Baghdad, Cordoba, and Cairo saw the establishment of libraries that housed collections of Quranic manuscripts. Rulers and wealthy patrons donated lavishly adorned copies, aiming to display both piety and cultural sophistication. Scholars frequented these libraries to compare recitations, examine commentaries, and produce further manuscripts for distribution.

14.10.2 Scriptoriums and Professional Scribes

Especially during the Abbasid period and onward, specialized workshops (scriptoriums) emerged, where professional scribes devoted themselves to producing Quranic codices. They worked under the supervision of calligraphy masters, who ensured consistency in style. Quality control processes included multiple reviews of completed sections to catch any transcription errors. The combination of artistic excellence and rigorous proofreading gave rise to manuscripts that were as accurate as they were beautiful.

14.10.3 Waqf (Endowments) for Quran Copies

Many wealthy Muslims set up waqf (charitable endowments) to fund the copying and dissemination of the Quran. Mosques, madrasas, and libraries benefited from these pious donations. This system reinforced the communal ethos of preserving the holy text for future generations. Copies produced under waqf were often placed in public spaces, accessible to anyone wishing to learn or recite. Through this philanthropic model, the tradition of Quranic scholarship was woven into the social and religious fabric of the empire.

14.11 Cultural Interactions and Script Evolution

14.11.1 Regional Stylistic Differences

As Muslims settled in Africa, Central Asia, and beyond, local aesthetics blended with Arabic calligraphy. In North Africa, angular Maghribi scripts emerged. In Ottoman Turkey, scripts like Thuluth and Naskh reached high artistic refinement. In Persian lands, the Nastaʿliq style eventually became predominant for non-Quranic works, though for the Quran itself Naskh or Thuluth remained standard. These cultural interactions showcased the adaptability of Arabic script while keeping the Quran's text inviolate.

14.11.2 Influence of Paper Manufacturing

Paper-making techniques, introduced from China in the 8th century, transformed manuscript production. By the 10th century, paper mills flourished in Baghdad, Damascus, and other centers. Paper was cheaper and easier to handle than parchment, allowing scribes to produce more copies of the Quran. This technological boost led to an increase in literacy, scholarly activity, and the further spread of Islamic literature. The Quran, being the most revered text, was among the first to be copied widely on paper.

14.11.3 Artistic Exchanges in Border Regions

In borderlands like al-Andalus (Muslim Spain) and the Silk Road routes through Central Asia, Muslim scribes encountered Byzantine, Visigothic, or Chinese artistic traditions. Ornamental motifs—like geometric patterns, arabesques, and calligraphic medallions—were integrated into Quranic manuscripts. These hybrid styles did not compromise textual integrity but enriched visual presentation, underscoring the universal message of the Quran through diverse artistic expressions.

Chapter Fifteen: The Umayyad Period and Quranic Developments

15.1 Introduction

The Umayyad Caliphate (661–750 CE) was the first hereditary dynasty in Islam, founded soon after the tumultuous period of the Rashidun Caliphs (Abu Bakr, Umar, Uthman, and Ali). Under the Umayyads, the Islamic realm stretched from the Iberian Peninsula in the west to parts of Central Asia in the east. This rapid expansion introduced Islam—and the Quran—to an even wider range of peoples, languages, and cultures. While political controversies were common, the Umayyads also oversaw administrative centralization, artistic achievements, and important developments in religious scholarship.

In this chapter, we will explore how Quranic studies and practices evolved during the Umayyad era. Building upon the standardized text established by Caliph Uthman, we will see how the empire's growth fueled the need for more robust teaching of the Quran, especially in newly conquered territories. We will examine the official policy on Quranic distribution, the rise of Quranic schools (kuttab), the introduction of basic diacritical marks, and the architectural expression of Quranic passages on structures like the Dome of the Rock. In addition, we will discuss how political dynamics—particularly the tension between the Umayyads and various opposition groups—influenced Quranic interpretation and recitation traditions. Although the Umayyads faced criticisms for their governance, they nonetheless played a pivotal role in shaping how the Muslim community engaged with the Quran for generations to come.

15.2 Establishment of Umayyad Rule

15.2.1 From the Aftermath of Ali's Death to Muawiyah's Accession

Following the assassination of Caliph Ali in 661 CE, the Muslim community found itself grappling with deep divisions. Ali's son Hasan briefly became caliph but soon renounced his claim, preferring a negotiated peace with Muawiyah ibn Abi Sufyan to avert further bloodshed. As a result, Muawiyah emerged as the uncontested leader, founding what became the Umayyad dynasty. He established Damascus as the capital, shifting the political center from Medina to Syria.

Muawiyah was known for his administrative acumen, having served as governor of Syria under previous caliphs. Although some Muslims questioned the legitimacy of hereditary succession, Muawiyah's skillful governance calmed immediate tensions. Still, resentment lingered among factions loyal to Ali's family (the proto-Shi'a) and the Kharijites. Despite these challenges, the empire, now consolidated under Umayyad control, was poised to expand further.

15.2.2 Hereditary Succession and Administrative Structures

One hallmark of Umayyad governance was the establishment of hereditary rule. Muawiyah designated his son Yazid as heir, setting a precedent for dynastic succession that stood in contrast to the earlier caliphates, where leadership was (in theory) based on community consensus. Over time, the Umayyads refined bureaucracy, appointing governors to provinces, organizing tax collection, and instituting administrative records (diwan).

In these provincial centers, the Quran assumed an administrative function as well: it was used to legitimize rule and underscore the caliph's religious authority. Umayyad officials built mosques and religious schools, ensuring that the standardized Uthmanic Mushaf accompanied their expanding realm. Although tensions existed, the Quran remained universally revered and helped unify diverse populations under the banner of Islam.

15.3 Quranic Education and Dissemination

15.3.1 Growth of Kuttab (Elementary Schools)

With an expanding empire came an influx of new converts, many of whom spoke languages other than Arabic—such as Berber in North Africa, various Iranian dialects in Persia, and local tongues in Transoxiana (Central Asia). To facilitate religious education, local communities established kuttab (elementary schools) where children (and sometimes adults) learned to recite the Quran, write basic Arabic script, and perform ritual practices like prayer.

The teaching at kuttab typically emphasized correct memorization and pronunciation, ensuring that even novices acquired at least rudimentary recitational skills. In some regions, advanced students proceeded to study with recognized ulama (scholars), deepening their knowledge of the Quran's meanings and classical Arabic grammar. The Umayyads often supported these schools by appointing teachers or providing endowments. Although the state's assistance varied, the network of kuttab became an informal but widespread means of transmitting the Quran across continents.

15.3.2 Establishment of Regional Teaching Circles

In major cities like Damascus, Kufa, Basra, and Fustat (in Egypt), specialized teaching circles emerged around respected companions or their students. These circles were not formal universities in the modern sense but functioned similarly to study groups. A senior scholar—often a companion or second-generation Muslim (tabi'un)—would recite the Quran and explain its verses. Pupils memorized what they heard, noted the teacher's commentary, and sometimes transcribed passages. This process helped standardize Quranic interpretation within a given lineage of scholarship.

For instance, in Kufa, traditions traced back to Abdullah ibn Mas'ud, while in Damascus, teachers might link their knowledge to Uthman's reciters. Although local recitation styles (qira'at) started to differentiate slightly, the basic content stayed consistent due to the unified Uthmanic script. By the close of the Umayyad period, each major city boasted a recognized school of Quranic study, planting the seeds for the formalization of the "Seven (or Ten) Qira'at" in the centuries to come.

15.3.3 Official Patronage and Mosque-Based Learning

Prominent Umayyad rulers, such as Abdul Malik ibn Marwan (685–705 CE) and his son Al-Walid (705–715 CE), sponsored large mosque constructions. Within these mosques, designated areas or annexes were set up for teaching Quranic recitation. This was especially apparent in the Great Mosque of Damascus, where state-appointed imams conducted lessons for the growing urban population. Similar patterns arose in cities like Qayrawan (in present-day Tunisia) and Cordoba (in al-Andalus), bridging distance and cultural barriers through a common scriptural focus.

15.4 Political Turmoil and the Quran

15.4.1 The Second Fitnah

Political unrest continued under the Umayyads. The Second Fitnah (680–692 CE) included the tragic event at Karbala in 680 CE, where Husayn ibn Ali (Ali's son and the Prophet's grandson) was killed by Umayyad forces. This event was a massive blow to supporters of the Ahl al-Bayt (the Prophet's family). The crisis also involved rival claimants to the caliphate, including Abd Allah ibn al-Zubayr in Mecca.

Although these conflicts dealt mainly with governance, both sides invoked Quranic verses to justify their claims. Ibn al-Zubayr's faction, for example, cited passages about opposing tyrannical rulers, whereas Umayyad loyalists appealed to verses about unity and obedience to authority. Despite such rhetorical battles, neither faction challenged the validity of the Uthmanic Mushaf or tried to alter it. The sacred text remained off-limits to political manipulation, even if verses were selectively quoted.

15.4.2 Abdullah ibn al-Zubayr's Governance in Mecca

From 683 to 692 CE, Ibn al-Zubayr controlled Mecca and declared himself caliph in opposition to the Umayyads. As the guardian of the Ka'bah, he sought to emphasize Mecca's religious primacy. He commissioned expansions and renovations of the sanctuary and promoted scholarly gatherings focusing on hadith and Quranic exegesis. Although his rule was eventually crushed by the Umayyad forces, the seeds of scholarship he nurtured influenced later studies of the Quran in the Hijaz region, reinforcing devotion to the holy text despite political upheaval.

15.4.3 The Dome of the Rock Inscriptions

One of the most enduring cultural legacies of the Umayyads was the construction of the Dome of the Rock in Jerusalem (completed around 691–692 CE under Caliph Abdul Malik). Its interior and exterior walls bear extensive Quranic passages, including verses that emphasize monotheism, refute the divinity of Jesus, and affirm Muhammad's prophethood. This architectural marvel, with its inscriptions, served multiple purposes: it celebrated Islam's supremacy in a city sacred to Jews and Christians, and it showcased the new empire's mastery of large-scale monumental art.

The Dome of the Rock inscriptions remain among the earliest surviving epigraphic evidence of Quranic text, providing scholars with valuable data on 7th-century Arabic script. While the wording aligns with the Uthmanic standard, the inscriptions show an early stage of letter shapes and occasional diacritical experimentation. This demonstrates that, even under political tension, the Umayyads invested in grand projects that broadcast the Quran's message.

15.5 Administration and Quranic Influence

15.5.1 Arabic as the Administrative Language

Under the Umayyads, particularly Abdul Malik, Arabic was established as the empire's official administrative language. Before this, local languages—Greek in Syria, Coptic in Egypt, and Persian in former Sasanian areas—were used in government offices. By switching to Arabic, the Umayyads not only unified bureaucratic processes but also exposed more non-Arabs to the language of the Quran. Over generations, populations from North Africa to Iran gradually adopted Arabic, easing their direct engagement with scripture.

15.5.2 Coinage and Quranic Phrases

Another innovation was the introduction of purely Islamic coinage. Earlier Muslim rulers had borrowed Byzantine or Sasanian coin designs. But during Abdul Malik's reign, coins were minted bearing Arabic inscriptions, often referencing Quranic statements about God's oneness (tawhid). Such coins, circulated throughout the empire, served as daily reminders of the faith's core message and displayed the new Islamic identity shaped under Umayyad rule.

15.5.3 Judicial Decisions and Quranic Law

Quranic guidance increasingly entered legal disputes under the Umayyads. While earlier caliphs sometimes administered justice directly, the expanding empire required a more formal court system. Qadis (judges) were appointed to rule based on the Quran and the Prophet's traditions. This nascent legal approach laid the foundation for later Islamic jurisprudence (fiqh). Although still not fully systematic—written law codes had yet to form—Quranic norms about contract law, inheritance, and punishment were visibly shaping daily governance.

15.6 Advancements in Quranic Orthography

15.6.1 Continuing Use of Kufic Script

Kufic remained the dominant style for Quranic manuscripts during most of the Umayyad period. Large, bold letters were favored for public readings in mosques, allowing listeners to follow the text at a distance. While earlier manuscripts had minimal decoration, scribes under the Umayyads began experimenting with occasional illumination—especially for surah headings. Still, the focus was primarily on clarity and uniformity with the Uthmanic standard.

15.6.2 Introduction of Basic Vowel Markings

As the empire absorbed many non-Arabs, basic diacritical aids were introduced to avoid misreadings of the Quran. Early markers might appear as red or yellow dots placed above or below letters, indicating short vowels or distinctions between similar letters. Although such markings were not as elaborate as the later systems, they represented a significant step in making the Quran more accessible to diverse communities. Over time, the practice of including these markings in official or teaching copies became standard.

15.6.3 Evidence from Umayyad-Era Fragments

Some surviving manuscript fragments—often found in mosque storerooms or discovered through archaeological excavations—show transitional features of orthography. For example, a page might have partial diacritics for certain challenging words but not for every letter. Spacing between words also varied, reflecting the scribes' attempts to balance aesthetics with readability. These fragments confirm that the consonantal skeleton of the text remained stable, even as notational practices evolved.

15.7 Sectarian Movements and Quranic Interpretation

15.7.1 Early Shi'a Communities

During Umayyad rule, Shi'a groups, especially in Iraq and Persia, maintained reverence for Ali's family. While they never contested the authenticity of Uthman's Mushaf, they often highlighted interpretive angles favoring Ahl al-Bayt. Some early Shi'a writings discussed how certain verses related to Ali's leadership or indicated the special status of the Prophet's household. Despite political tensions, mainstream Shi'a scholars continued to read and memorize the same standard Quranic text as the rest of the ummah, albeit with distinct commentary.

15.7.2 Kharijite Approaches

Kharijites, though diminished in numbers after heavy crackdowns by the Umayyads, continued to exist in pockets of Arabia, North Africa, and Persia. Their communities insisted on strict obedience to the Quran, leading to literalist interpretations of certain verses about sin and punishment. Yet, like other groups, they recognized the Uthmanic text as binding. The differences arose primarily in how they applied the scripture to political and moral issues.

15.7.3 Qadariyya, Jabriyya, and Early Theological Debates

Another aspect of Quranic interpretation surfaced in early theological discussions about free will and predestination. Groups known as Qadariyya emphasized human free agency, using verses suggesting moral responsibility, while Jabriyya (or fatalists) pointed to verses underscoring God's absolute power over destiny. Although these debates were still relatively small in scope compared to later centuries, they highlighted how Muslims turned to the Quran for resolving profound existential questions. The Umayyad authorities generally discouraged such speculative theology, fearing it could fuel political dissent, but the intellectual seeds were sown for future theological schools.

15.8 Architectural Celebrations of the Quran

15.8.1 Mosque Construction Boom

The Umayyads embarked on a grand program of mosque building, transforming or expanding cityscapes to reflect Islamic identity. The Great Mosque of Damascus, completed under Al-Walid, stood as a major symbol of the empire's architectural might. Its interior included Quranic inscriptions and decorative motifs consistent with Islamic aniconism. Similar expansions in Mosul, Basra, Kufa, and Fustat solidified the mosque as not just a place of worship but a communal center where the Quran was recited, taught, and publicly displayed.

15.8.2 Dome of the Rock Revisited

While already mentioned, the Dome of the Rock warrants emphasis as it epitomized the Umayyad approach to religious art. The extensive Quranic passages integrated into its walls—some of the earliest known epigraphic records—demonstrated how the empire sought to proclaim Islam's theology openly in a contested sacred space (Jerusalem). The script used in these inscriptions is an early form of Kufic, reflective of the period's transitional orthographic style.

15.8.3 Inscriptions as Public Proclamation

Beyond mosques, the Umayyads often employed Quranic verses on milestones, coins, and public buildings. For instance, certain city gates might feature a verse extolling the unity of God or urging believers to remain steadfast. These inscriptions served as a form of political communication, subtly reminding subjects of the empire's Islamic ethos. They underscored the idea that the caliphate was guided by the same revelation central to every Muslim's faith.

15.9 Towards the End of Umayyad Rule

15.9.1 Social Unease and Revolts

Despite military success and cultural patronage, social dissatisfaction brewed among non-Arab converts (mawali), who resented second-class treatment, and among Arabs in far-flung provinces frustrated by Umayyad tax policies. Coupled with the continuous claim of Ali's family to rightful leadership, these tensions created the conditions for rebellion. The Abbasids harnessed such resentments in a revolutionary movement that culminated in overthrowing the Umayyads in 750 CE.

15.9.2 Preservation of the Quranic Heritage

Even as revolts destabilized the state, the Quranic heritage remained a unifying factor. Neither the Abbasid revolutionaries nor the Umayyads' supporters considered altering the scripture. Qurans circulated across the empire with the same fundamental text, and teachers, reciters, and scribes continued their tasks. Political change did not disturb the bedrock of the religion: the Uthmanic Mushaf with its recognized orthography.

15.9.3 Legacy of Umayyad Patronage

When the Abbasids took power, they inherited a vast domain already infused with Quranic instruction, standard manuscripts, and a rudimentary system of diacritical aids. They built upon the educational and architectural foundations laid by the Umayyads. Quranic manuscripts from the Umayyad period provided a template for the next generation of scribes. Similarly, the official uses of the Quran in inscriptions, coinage, and public ceremony influenced how subsequent rulers displayed their piety and legitimacy.

Chapter Sixteen: The Abbasid Period and Rise of Quranic Scholarship

16.1 Introduction

In 750 CE, the Abbasid revolution toppled the Umayyads, ushering in a new era in Islamic history. Under the Abbasids (750–1258 CE), the caliphate shifted its capital to Baghdad, transforming it into a cultural, scientific, and intellectual powerhouse. This period, often referred to as the Islamic "Golden Age," witnessed remarkable achievements in science, philosophy, literature, and religious studies. Central to these pursuits was the Quran, whose study assumed unprecedented depth and sophistication.

In this chapter, we explore how the Abbasids built upon the Quranic foundations laid by the Rashidun and Umayyad eras to develop advanced scholarship in areas such as tafsir (exegesis), qira'at (recitation modes), and Arabic grammar. We will examine the establishment of institutions, patronage for scholars, and the interplay between the Quran and broader intellectual currents—such as Greek-inspired rationalism (falsafa) and local interpretive traditions. Despite political challenges and eventual fragmentation of Abbasid authority, the scholarly legacy concerning the Quran thrived, solidifying interpretive structures that endure in Islamic thought.

16.2 The Abbasid Ascendancy

16.2.1 Overthrow of the Umayyads

Discontent among Persian mawali, Shi'a sympathizers, and various Arab tribes fueled the Abbasid revolt. Abu al-Abbas as-Saffah emerged as the first Abbasid caliph in 750 CE after defeating the last Umayyad ruler, Marwan II. The Abbasids claimed legitimate descent from the Prophet's uncle, al-Abbas, positioning themselves as champions of a more inclusive Islamic polity. They moved the capital to Baghdad, strategically located near older Persian centers, which welcomed the new regime.

16.2.2 The Cosmopolitan Capital of Baghdad

Under the early Abbasids—especially caliphs like al-Mansur (754–775 CE), Harun al-Rashid (786–809 CE), and al-Ma'mun (813–833 CE)—Baghdad blossomed into one of the largest and most cosmopolitan cities of its time. Trade routes converged there, bringing scholars, merchants, and ideas from across Asia, Africa, and Europe. This confluence enriched the environment for Quranic studies, as a wide spectrum of linguistic and cultural backgrounds engaged in learning. Patronage of learning by the caliphs fostered vibrant debates on theology, law, and exegesis.

16.2.3 Integrating Persian Influences

The Abbasids benefited from Persian administrative traditions, adopting refined bureaucratic practices that streamlined governance. Many Persian families, once marginalized under the Umayyads, gained influence in the Abbasid court. This shift also impacted religious scholarship: Persian intellectual culture, which prized scholarship and debate, combined with Arab devotion to the Quranic text, generating a fertile ground for advanced studies in language, grammar, and commentary.

16.3 Patronage of Islamic Scholarship

16.3.1 Libraries and Academies

One of the hallmark features of the Abbasid golden age was the establishment of extensive libraries and research institutions, the most famous being the Bayt al-Hikmah (House of Wisdom) in Baghdad. While primarily known for translating Greek and Persian works into Arabic, these centers also housed extensive collections of Quranic manuscripts and tafsir writings. Scholars and scribes had access to a breadth of knowledge under one roof, stimulating cross-disciplinary engagement—from hadith studies to astronomy.

16.3.2 The Caliph's Support of Scholars

Abbasid caliphs, especially Harun al-Rashid and his son al-Ma'mun, were known for lavishly funding scholars. While their patronage often focused on philosophy, mathematics, and medicine, it also encompassed religious sciences. Eminent mufassirun (Quranic exegetes), grammarians, and reciters benefited from state stipends or official appointments. This institutional backing enabled them to dedicate themselves full-time to writing commentaries, preserving qira'at traditions, and refining Arabic grammar rules to facilitate accurate Quranic interpretation.

16.3.3 Court Debates and Public Assemblies

In Baghdad and other major cities, the courts of rulers and governors sometimes hosted majalis (gatherings) where scholars presented arguments on theological or legal matters. The Quran often stood at the center of these debates. Whether the issue involved theological intricacies about God's attributes or practical fiqh questions, participants would quote verses and interpret them with methods shaped by earlier traditions. These assemblies elevated the Quran's public profile, as each faction strove to present the most compelling reading of the text.

16.4 Development of Tafsir (Quranic Exegesis)

16.4.1 Early Exegetical Efforts

Before the Abbasids, companions and tabi'un had laid a foundation for tafsir through oral commentary. Certain companion-based traditions (e.g., from Ibn Abbas, Ubayy ibn Ka'b, and Ali ibn Abi Talib) circulated in teaching circles. The earliest known written tafsir, often attributed to Mujahid ibn Jabr (d. 722 CE) or Muhammad ibn Ka'b al-Qurazi, was relatively concise. It presented transmissions on the reasons behind verse revelations and basic lexical clarifications.

16.4.2 The Emergence of Classical Tafsir

Under Abbasid patronage, scholars compiled these oral traditions into more extensive exegetical works. Among the most influential was the tafsir of Ibn Jarir al-Tabari (d. 923 CE). Although he lived after the Abbasid golden age had peaked, he represented the culmination of centuries of scholarship. His Jami' al-Bayan 'an Ta'wil Ay al-Qur'an systematically organized earlier transmissions, weighed their authenticity, and provided linguistic, historical, and theological explanations. Al-Tabari's method exemplified the Abbasid inclination for thorough, organized scholarship, capturing a wide range of interpretive voices.

16.4.3 Different Schools of Tafsir

By the 9th century, distinct schools of tafsir methodology emerged. One line, often called tafsir bi'l-ma'thur (exegesis based on transmitted reports), heavily relied on companion statements and hadith. Another line, tafsir bi'l-ra'y (exegesis based on reasoned opinion), allowed scholars to engage with the text through linguistic analysis and rational argument, though still anchored by the text and the Prophet's tradition. Prominent scholars integrated both approaches, balancing respect for transmitted knowledge with reasoned interpretation that accounted for grammar, rhetoric, and context.

16.5 Advances in Arabic Grammar and Linguistics

16.5.1 The Need for Codified Grammar

As Arabic spread beyond its native heartlands, preserving the correct recitation of the Quran became a priority. Scholars feared that "linguistic corruption" (lahn) might creep in if grammar rules were not standardized. Building upon earlier grammarians like Abu al-Aswad al-Du'ali, Abbasid-era luminaries such as Sibawayh (d. circa 796 CE) composed groundbreaking works like Al-Kitab, the earliest systematic treatise on Arabic grammar.

16.5.2 Sibawayh and the Basran School

Sibawayh, a Persian by origin, studied in Basra under influential teachers. Al-Kitab analyzed sentence structure, morphology, and phonology in detail, providing examples often drawn from the Quran. It helped unify grammatical concepts across the empire, ensuring that advanced students of the Quran could parse verses correctly. The Basran school became known for its rigorous approach and would later rival the Kufan school in debates over grammatical interpretations and usage.

16.5.3 Impact on Quranic Interpretation

A firm grasp of grammar was deemed essential for any serious mufassir (exegete). Subtle differences in case endings, word order, or morphological forms could yield distinct theological or legal implications. Abbasid grammarians cross-referenced the Quranic text to illustrate grammatical principles, while exegetes consulted grammar treatises to confirm their readings. This synergy meant that the study of the Quran and the study of Arabic grammar reinforced each other, elevating the precision with which scholars interpreted divine revelation.

16.6 The Formalization of Qira'at (Recitation Modes)

16.6.1 Canonical Recitation Traditions

Although recognized modes of Quranic recitation predated the Abbasids, it was during this era that scholars like Abu Bakr ibn Mujahid (d. 324 AH / 936 CE) systematically categorized them. He identified seven canonical readings, each linked to a prominent reciter and their chain of transmission—for instance, Nafi' in Medina, Ibn Kathir in Mecca, 'Asim in Kufa, Hamzah in Kufa, al-Kisa'i in Kufa, Abu 'Amr in Basra, and Ibn 'Amir in Syria. Later scholars added three more, making it ten canonical qira'at overall.

16.6.2 Establishment of Criteria for Authenticity

Ibn Mujahid and his contemporaries developed rigorous criteria for accepting a recitation as canonical:

1. **Uninterrupted Chain of Transmission**: Each reading had to be traced back reliably to the Prophet's companions.
2. **Conformity to Uthman's Mushaf**: The recitation could not conflict with the consonantal skeleton of the standard text.
3. **Phonetic Consistency**: The reading had to match accepted rules of Arabic phonology and grammar.

Only recitations meeting these criteria were endorsed as legitimate. This formal recognition protected the Quran from being diluted by spurious variants, ensuring fidelity to the earliest modes the Prophet allowed.

16.6.3 Teaching and Preservation

Each canonical qira'ah was preserved through designated lines of transmitters (riwayat). For instance, the recitation of 'Asim was commonly transmitted via Shu'bah or Hafs. Under Abbasid support, reciters traveled or wrote treatises to spread these authoritative traditions. Institutions in Baghdad, Kufa, Basra, and other centers set up specialized classes, awarding certificates (ijazah) to students who achieved mastery. This structure integrated seamlessly with the broader scholarly networks supported by caliphal patronage.

16.7 Theological Debates and the Quran

16.7.1 The Mihna (Inquisition) on the Quran's Createdness

One of the most dramatic episodes in Abbasid religious history was the Mihna (833–848 CE), introduced by Caliph al-Ma'mun and continued by his successors al-Mu'tasim and al-Wathiq. Influenced by Mu'tazilite theology, which emphasized rationalism, the caliphs decreed that the Quran was "created" rather than "co-eternal with God." Scholars who refused this creed risked imprisonment or punishment.

Ahmad ibn Hanbal (d. 855 CE), a leading traditionalist scholar, famously resisted, enduring imprisonment but refusing to declare the Quran created. Over time, public and scholarly support for the Mu'tazilite position waned. Caliph al-Mutawakkil eventually ended the Mihna, endorsing the more traditional view that the Quran was the uncreated word of God. Though the dispute focused on theology rather than the text itself, it highlighted how deeply the Abbasids were involved in shaping religious discourse. The content of the Quran was not in question, but its ontological status sparked intense controversy.

16.7.2 Impact on Sunni Orthodoxy

The Mihna solidified the position of scholars like Ahmad ibn Hanbal, who championed a strict adherence to hadith-based interpretations and resisted philosophical or rational intrusions into scripture. This stance grew into what became known as the Hanbali school of Islamic law, influential in shaping Sunni orthodoxy. Subsequent generations saw a diminished role for Mu'tazilite theology, though rationalistic tendencies continued in other forms (like the Ash'ari school). Throughout these debates, the authority of the Quran's text remained unchallenged; the dispute lay in how to articulate divine attributes consistent with revealed scripture.

16.7.3 Shi'a Theology and Tafsir

During the Abbasid era, various Shi'a groups developed more elaborate theologies, often focusing on the authority of the Imams as interpreters of the

Quran. Twelver Shi'ism, for instance, revered a line of twelve Imams from Ali onward, viewing them as divinely guided exegetes. Though the majority of Shi'a also accepted the same Uthmanic codex, they sometimes posited deeper esoteric interpretations, particularly relating to the spiritual significance of the Imamate. These Shi'a exegetical works circulated in Abbasid territories, though they remained outside the Sunni mainstream.

16.8 Literary and Linguistic Achievements Influenced by the Quran

16.8.1 Flourishing of Adab (Literature)

The Quran's eloquence and moral themes inspired Muslim authors to produce literary works known collectively as adab—encompassing poetry, prose, ethics, and historical narratives. Many of these works were peppered with Quranic quotations or allusions, reflecting the central role scripture played in public life. Writers like al-Jahiz (d. 868/869 CE) in Basra, famed for his wit and linguistic skill, repeatedly referenced Quranic phrases, recognizing how deeply they resonated with Arabic-speaking audiences.

16.8.2 Influence on Poetry

Although poetry had been central in pre-Islamic Arabia, the emergence of Islam introduced new themes and influences. While some Abbasid poets wrote panegyric verses extolling caliphs, others composed mystical or devotional poetry referencing Quranic narratives. Al-Mutanabbi (d. 965 CE), though primarily concerned with praising patrons, also wove Quranic imagery into his verses. Likewise, early Sufi poets, before the formal crystallization of Sufism, used Quranic metaphors for devotion, love of God, and moral reflection.

16.8.3 Grammar and Lexicography for the Quran

Expanding on earlier achievements, Abbasid scholars produced comprehensive lexicons that explained Quranic vocabulary in detail. Works like Al-Ayn by al-Khalil ibn Ahmad (d. 786 CE) and subsequent dictionaries helped unify Arabic usage, a boon for non-native speakers. These lexicons often cited Quranic verses to exemplify word meanings, ensuring that even advanced philological scholarship was anchored in scripture.

16.9 Further Refinements in Manuscript Production

16.9.1 Transition from Kufic to Naskh

While Kufic script dominated the early Abbasid period, from the 9th century onward, Naskh began to gain favor for copying Qurans. Naskh's flowing form and clearer distinctions between letters made it easier to read, especially once fully vowelled. By the 10th and 11th centuries, most standard-sized Quranic manuscripts were penned in refined Naskh, though Kufic persisted for monumental or decorative inscriptions.

16.9.2 Gold Illumination and Ornamental Art

Wealthy Abbasid patrons sponsored lavishly illuminated Qurans, featuring intricate geometric and arabesque designs in gold leaf. Surah headings might be placed inside cartouches embellished with vibrant pigments. Skilled calligraphers such as Ibn Muqla (d. 940 CE) and Ibn al-Bawwab (d. 1022 CE) perfected proportional scripts, shaping the aesthetic that influenced subsequent centuries of Islamic calligraphy. These manuscripts showcased the high regard in which Muslims held the physical form of the Quran, while always preserving the same textual content.

16.9.3 Spread of Paper Manufacture

During Abbasid rule, paper-making spread from China through Central Asia to the Middle East, drastically reducing costs compared to parchment. By the 9th century, paper mills operated in Baghdad and other cities, enabling the production of more Quranic manuscripts than ever before. This growth facilitated broader dissemination: scholars could produce multiple copies, educational institutions could maintain library stocks, and private collectors could own personal Mushafs. The synergy of improved script, abundant paper, and calligraphic skill contributed to a golden era of manuscript production.

16.10 Regional Variations and the Abbasid Decline

16.10.1 Provincial Dynasties

From the 9th century onward, the Abbasids gradually lost direct control over distant provinces. Independent or semi-independent dynasties, such as the Aghlabids in North Africa, the Saffarids and Samanids in Persia, and the Tulunids and Ikhshidids in Egypt, emerged. Yet each local power recognized the sanctity of the same Uthmanic Quran. They, too, funded mosques, sponsored scribes, and cultivated religious scholars who adhered to canonical qira'at and mainstream tafsir traditions.

16.10.2 The Buyid and Seljuk Interventions

By the 10th and 11th centuries, Persian Shi'a dynasties like the Buyids seized Baghdad, while later the Sunni Seljuks gained influence, overshadowing the Abbasid caliphs. Still, the spiritual centrality of the Quran transcended political transformations. Rulers continued to rely on religious legitimacy by upholding the recognized text. The caliph, though weakened, remained a symbolic protector of orthodoxy, especially in maintaining scriptural continuity.

16.10.3 Intellectual Continuity

Despite fractionalization, the chain of scholarship remained largely unbroken. Students continued traveling to major centers—Baghdad, Nishapur, Cairo, Damascus—to study with leading Quranic reciters and exegetes. The entire region thus remained part of a shared intellectual realm, bound by reverence for the Quran's words. Political fragmentation did not lead to textual fragmentation; the same Mushaf guided believers from Cordoba to Samarqand, thanks to centuries of meticulous preservation.

16.11 Lasting Contributions of the Abbasid Era

16.11.1 Institutionalizing Quranic Sciences

One of the Abbasids' greatest achievements was the formalization of Quranic sciences (ulum al-Quran). This umbrella term covered tafsir, qira'at, asbab al-nuzul (occasions of revelation), nasikh wa mansukh (abrogation), and more. Scholars wrote specialized treatises on each branch. By the end of the Abbasid golden age, a serious student could pursue a structured course of study in these disciplines, earning recognition as a faqih (jurisconsult) or mufassir (exegete).

16.11.2 Integration with Broader Fields of Learning

Unlike in some societies, religious and "secular" sciences were not rigidly separated. Mathematicians like al-Khwarizmi, philosophers like al-Kindi and al-Farabi, and physicians like Ibn Sina all lived in a milieu where the Quran was the spiritual wellspring. Some wrote theological treatises that began with praise of God, referencing Quranic verses, before delving into geometry or logic. The unity of knowledge—rooted in a shared scriptural worldview—defined the Abbasid intellectual climate.

16.11.3 Influence on Future Islamic Civilizations

Even after the Mongols sacked Baghdad in 1258 CE, the scholarly traditions honed under Abbasid patronage continued. Regions like Mamluk Egypt, Timurid Persia, and Ottoman Anatolia carried forward the Abbasid legacy of Quranic scholarship. They inherited well-organized methods for teaching recitation, standard reference works for grammar, compiled tafsir texts, and the best practices for copying and preserving the Mushaf. The foundation laid during the Abbasid era thus shaped Islamic civilization far beyond the caliphate's formal demise.

Chapter Seventeen: Major Early Scholars of the Quran

17.1 Introduction

Over the first few centuries of Islamic history, a number of scholars emerged whose devotion to studying, teaching, and interpreting the Quran shaped the course of Muslim civilization. Building on the work of the Prophet Muhammad's companions, these pioneers clarified the text's recitation, explained its meanings, and established rigorous methods for verifying authenticity. While previous chapters have touched on some prominent figures in passing, this chapter concentrates more fully on the individuals who laid enduring foundations for Quranic scholarship, from the era of the tabi'un (successors to the companions) through the early Abbasid period.

In particular, we will highlight those who contributed to **Quranic exegesis (tafsir)**, **recitation (qira'at)**, and the emergent science of **Arabic grammar** specifically tailored to safeguarding the text. We will also discuss how these scholars' teachings were preserved, the role of their personal character and ethical conduct in inspiring students, and the ways in which regional dynamics (e.g., in Mecca, Medina, Kufa, Basra, Syria, and beyond) influenced their approach to understanding the Quran. By studying these major early scholars, we gain insights into the human element behind a tradition that, while ultimately grounded in divine revelation, relied on dedicated intellects and sincere hearts to maintain and transmit the Quran's message accurately.

17.2 The Tabi'un and Their Role in Early Transmission

17.2.1 Definition and Importance of the Tabi'un

The term **tabi'un** refers to the generation of Muslims who did not meet the Prophet Muhammad directly but studied under his companions. They stand as a historical bridge between the era of revelation and the more structured scholarship that emerged in subsequent centuries. Many of the tabi'un specialized in **memorizing** the Quran and recounting the **asbab al-nuzul** (occasions of revelation) transmitted by companions. They also gathered the companions' teachings about the correct interpretation of difficult or ambiguous verses.

Notably, the tabi'un served as the earliest teachers in key Islamic centers. As expansions continued under the Rashidun and early Umayyad caliphs, these men and women traveled to newly founded cities or existing hubs—like Kufa, Basra, and Fustat—bringing direct lines of instruction from the companions. From them, we get the earliest expositions on how to read and understand particular surahs. Their closeness to the companions meant their teachings were considered highly authoritative by subsequent generations.

17.2.2 Exemplary Figures Among the Tabi'un

A few representative individuals from this generation:

- **Sa'id ibn al-Musayyib** (d. circa 94 AH / 712 CE): Based in Medina, he was regarded for his deep knowledge of both Quranic matters and Prophetic traditions. He conveyed many interpretive clarifications he had learned from companions such as Umar ibn al-Khattab and A'ishah.
- **'Alqamah ibn Qays** (d. circa 62 AH / 682 CE): A student of Abdullah ibn Mas'ud in Kufa, 'Alqamah retained much of Ibn Mas'ud's recitation style and exegesis. His meticulous approach helped establish Kufa as a center for Quranic scholarship focused on the traditions of Ibn Mas'ud.
- **Mujahid ibn Jabr** (d. 104 AH / 722 CE): Active in Mecca, Mujahid studied extensively with Ibn Abbas. He is often credited with producing one of the earliest systematic commentaries on the Quran (though in a simpler form than later tafsirs). His work paid close attention to linguistic nuances, reflecting Ibn Abbas's emphasis on clarifying the text's vocabulary and historical context.

Such figures ensured that the interpretive approaches of the companions were not lost, collecting them in embryonic "tafsir notebooks" or transmitting them orally to the next generation.

17.3 Pioneers of Quranic Exegesis (Tafsir)

17.3.1 Ibn Abbas: The "Interpreter of the Quran"

Among the companions themselves, **Abdullah ibn Abbas** (d. 68 AH / 687 CE) stands out as a towering figure in Quranic interpretation. Nicknamed **Habr al-Ummah** ("the scholar of the ummah") and **Tarjuman al-Quran** ("the interpreter of the Quran"), Ibn Abbas was closely related to the Prophet (his cousin) and learned from him directly while still young. After the Prophet's death, he traveled widely, collecting knowledge from senior companions and synthesizing their insights into a coherent approach to tafsir.

Ibn Abbas's exegetical style balanced literal explanation with contextual knowledge of events that led to a verse's revelation. His students—like Mujahid, Ikrimah, and Tawus—spread his teachings throughout the Muslim world. Even centuries later, major commentators (such as al-Tabari) frequently cite "Ibn Abbas said…" as a gold standard for explaining verses. Although he predated the formal "schools" of tafsir, Ibn Abbas's legacy shaped how subsequent generations approached interpretive questions, from grammar and vocabulary to theological implications.

17.3.2 Al-Hasan al-Basri and His Moral Emphasis

Al-Hasan al-Basri (d. 110 AH / 728 CE) was a tabi'i revered in Basra for his piety, eloquence, and moral teachings. Though best known for his ascetic perspective and ethical sermons, he also contributed significantly to Quranic interpretation. Hasan al-Basri's tafsir sessions in the Basra mosque attracted large crowds. He integrated the textual explications handed down from companions with exhortations on piety, repentance, and reliance on God.

Hasan's approach to the Quran was not just academic; he emphasized how each verse should transform the believer's character. While his immediate commentary was less systematically recorded than that of some others, his moral-laden interpretations influenced later Sufi-leaning exegeses. Hasan also confronted theological dilemmas in the early Umayyad period, sometimes cautioning against over-politicizing the scripture. His balanced stance underscored that the Quran guides both personal spirituality and communal ethics.

17.3.3 Ibrahim al-Nakha'i and the Kufan Tradition

Kufa in Iraq produced a notable strand of Quranic scholarship tied closely to the companion Abdullah ibn Mas'ud. Among the later Kufan luminaries was **Ibrahim** al-Nakha'i (d. circa 96 AH / 715 CE), known for continuing the tradition of textual study combined with careful legal reasoning (fiqh). He inherited from Ibn Mas'ud's circle a preference for certain readings of ambiguous verses, as well as an emphasis on verifying interpretations through multiple chains of transmission.

Ibrahim's fiqh orientation led him to read the Quran not just for spiritual insight but also for legal rulings on inheritance, marriage, and financial transactions. Many subsequent Hanafi jurists considered themselves intellectually descended from al-Nakha'i, bridging exegesis and jurisprudence. This interweaving of Quranic commentary with practical law set a precedent for Sunni madhhab (school of law) developments under the Abbasids.

17.4 Founders of Qira'at Traditions

17.4.1 The Seven (and Ten) Imams of Recitation

While Chapter Sixteen discussed how canonical recitations (qira'at) were codified under Abbasid scholars like Ibn Mujahid, the actual founders of these traditions lived somewhat earlier. They were recognized as Imams of recitation in their respective cities, teaching thousands of students who then passed on their methods. A few are especially notable:

1. **Nafi' al-Madani** (d. 169 AH / 785 CE): Associated with Medina, Nafi''s recitation was known for its clear enunciation and mild elongations of vowels. His style was favored among many in the Hijaz.
2. **Ibn Kathir al-Makki** (d. 120 AH / 737 CE): Operating in Mecca, Ibn Kathir's approach integrated older recitation practices from the Prophet's companions who stayed near the Ka'bah.
3. **Abu 'Amr ibn al-'Ala'** (d. 154 AH / 770 CE): A Basran master of grammar and philology, Abu 'Amr's reading emphasized linguistic precision. He played a crucial role in bridging the fields of grammar and recitation.
4. **Asim ibn Abi al-Nujud** (d. 127 AH / 745 CE): Based in Kufa, Asim's recitation eventually became one of the most widespread, especially through the riwayah (transmission) of Hafs ibn Sulayman in later centuries.

5. **Ibn 'Amir al-Dimashqi** (d. 118 AH / 736 CE): A key authority in Damascus, Ibn 'Amir's readings reflected local traditions descending from Uthman's reciters in Syria.
6. **Hamzah al-Zayyat** (d. 156 AH / 772 CE) and **al-Kisa'i** (d. 189 AH / 805 CE): Both from Kufa, they refined earlier Kufan recitation methods, with al-Kisa'i also known for his advanced grammar scholarship.

These figures set the stage for the recognized canonical recitations: each reciter's tradition had unique phonetic traits—like how to pronounce hamzah, elongate vowels, or handle assimilations of letters—yet all conformed to the same basic Uthmanic consonantal text.

17.4.2 Methods of Transmission and Verification

The key to preserving these qira'at was rigorous teaching. A student had to recite the entire Quran under a master's supervision, demonstrating perfect reproduction of each verse's phonetic rules. The master would only grant **ijazah** (formal authorization) once fully satisfied. Chains of transmission were meticulously recorded, linking each reciter back to the founding imam and ultimately to the companions.

Early masters like Nafi' or Asim often taught for decades, maintaining daily sessions in mosques where novices and advanced pupils alike would recite. They prized consistent daily recitation: a teacher might ask a student to recite from memory large portions each morning, verifying both the melodic style and exact letter articulation. This disciplined environment ensured that any accidental innovation or drift from the recognized tradition was quickly corrected.

17.4.3 Integration with Local Cultures

As the empire stretched into North Africa, Persia, and beyond, some qira'at gained traction in specific regions. For instance, Nafi''s recitation (later transmitted by Warsh) became prevalent in North Africa. Meanwhile, Asim's recitation via Hafs spread widely in Iraq and eventually dominated many parts of the Muslim world. The existence of different recitations did not fracture the ummah's unity; rather, it enriched the tapestry of worship, so long as each style remained within the bounds of the Uthmanic text and possessed authentic chains to recognized early masters.

17.5 Grammarians and Lexicographers in Service of the Quran

17.5.1 Al-Khalil ibn Ahmad al-Farahidi

Al-Khalil ibn Ahmad (d. circa 170 AH / 786 CE) was a Basran scholar whose work profoundly influenced Arabic linguistic studies. Best known for compiling **Kitab al-'Ayn**, the earliest systematic dictionary of the Arabic language, Khalil identified and categorized roots alphabetically, clarifying many Quranic terms' nuances. His interest in metrics also led to the systematization of Arabic poetry's meters, which indirectly helped define rhythmic aspects relevant to Quranic recitation.

Although Khalil's direct commentaries on Quranic verses are sparse, his lexical achievements armed tafsir scholars with robust linguistic tools. By referencing al-'Ayn, an exegete could confirm a particular word's morphological patterns or synonyms, ensuring a more accurate reading of the Quran. Khalil's methodical approach exemplified how the impetus to understand scripture propelled advanced philological research.

17.5.2 Sibawayh and Al-Kitab

As discussed, **Sibawayh** (d. circa 180 AH / 796 CE) authored **Al-Kitab**, the foundational treatise of Arabic grammar. In it, he cited many Quranic examples to illustrate grammatical rules and morphological forms. Although Sibawayh did not produce a formal tafsir, his grammatical framework underpinned future commentary. For instance, an exegete might turn to Al-Kitab to resolve ambiguities in case endings that affect interpretive meaning (e.g., subject vs. object).

Sibawayh's reliance on Quranic evidence underscores how the text served as a cornerstone for standardizing the language. He also referenced pre-Islamic poetry, recognized for its eloquence, but gave the Quran precedence as the ultimate exemplar of correct Arabic usage. Later grammarians—al-Farra', al-Mubarrad, and Ibn Jinni—followed in Sibawayh's footsteps, ensuring that each grammatical rule aligned with possible Quranic forms.

17.5.3 Al-Farra' and the Kufa Tradition

Al-Farra' (d. 207 AH / 822 CE) represented the Kufan school of grammar, offering another perspective that sometimes differed from Basran orthodoxy. In works like **Ma'ani al-Quran**, he analyzed the stylistic and syntactic features of Quranic verses, striving to show how each variant reading fit recognized linguistic standards. This advanced the conversation between grammar specialists and reciters: was a certain reading accepted grammatically, or did it stretch the rules?

Al-Farra's analyses, deeply rooted in Kufa's heritage, often defended alternative grammatical interpretations that Basrans might reject, thereby legitimizing the diversity of recognized recitations. His approach exemplified the collegial rivalry between Basran and Kufan grammarians, both of whom anchored their arguments in the revered text of the Quran.

17.6 Early Commentators Who Shaped Classical Tafsir

17.6.1 Sufyan al-Thawri

Sufyan al-Thawri (d. 161 AH / 778 CE), primarily known as a hadith scholar and founder of a short-lived fiqh school, also offered Quranic commentaries. Though not systematically preserved like al-Tabari's, Sufyan's tafsir remarks circulated through his students in Kufa. He interpreted verses with an eye to ascetic piety and moral rectitude, echoing the approach of Hasan al-Basri. Sufyan's humility and devotion to worship lent credibility to his exegesis, which often emphasized the spiritual transformations the Quran should spark in believers' hearts.

17.6.2 'Abd al-Razzaq and Ibn Abi Shaybah

'Abd al-Razzaq al-San'ani (d. 211 AH / 827 CE) and **Ibn Abi Shaybah** (d. 235 AH / 849 CE) compiled large musannaf works—collections of hadith, rulings, and partial tafsir traditions. These compilations included chapters devoted to explaining certain Quranic verses. While not classical commentaries in the sense of continuous verse-by-verse exegesis, they preserved valuable remarks from early authorities. Through these collections, later scholars gleaned raw material for constructing fuller tafsir treatises.

17.6.3 Dawud al-Zahiri and Literalism

Dawud ibn 'Ali al-Zahiri (d. 270 AH / 884 CE) founded the Zahiri school of thought, known for strict textual literalism in law and interpretation. In his approach to the Quran, Dawud insisted that verses be taken primarily at face value unless a compelling textual reason mandated metaphorical reading. Although his school never attained the prominence of Hanafi, Maliki, Shafi'i, or Hanbali madhhabs, the Zahiri perspective influenced interpretive debates. By championing a literal reading, Dawud's stance forced other exegetes to articulate more clearly the principles guiding figurative or contextual interpretations. Thus, he contributed to the broader intellectual environment that honed exegetical rigor.

17.7 Ethos and Methodologies of Early Scholars

17.7.1 Verification (Tahqiq) and Chains of Transmission (Isnad)

A consistent theme among Quranic scholars was **tahqiq**—the drive to ensure accurate knowledge via established chains of transmission. Whether memorizing recitation modes or collecting companion statements about a verse's meaning, early scholars demanded robust isnad. This approach paralleled the hadith sciences, where each narrator's reliability was examined. Such vigilance helped prevent the infiltration of spurious interpretations.

17.7.2 Balancing Reason and Revelation

While reasoned analysis was encouraged, especially for grammar and linguistic details, the overarching ethos held that the Quran was God's word, deserving deference. Many early scholars warned against **excessive** speculative exegesis, mindful of the Prophet's caution against speaking about the Quran without knowledge. Conversely, they recognized the text's depth warranted thoughtful reflection. This balance between caution and inquiry formed the hallmark of mainstream Sunni scholarship: a readiness to engage logically with the text, but always anchored in transmitted knowledge from the Prophet and his companions.

17.7.3 Ethical Conduct of Scholars

The personal character of early scholars was often seen as part and parcel of their scholarship's credibility. Dedication to worship, humility, avoidance of worldly excess, and generosity were recurring traits admired in luminaries like Hasan al-Basri or Sufyan al-Thawri. Students typically sought not just knowledge from them, but also moral exemplars who lived by the Quranic ethics they taught. This model of the **'alim** (scholar) who was also a **zahid** (ascetic) or a devout worshipper solidified the spiritual authority that accompanied their intellectual contributions.

17.8 Regional Schools and Their Interchange

17.8.1 Medina: Legacy of Ibn Umar and Zayd ibn Thabit

Medina, the city of the Prophet, retained its preeminent position thanks to companions such as **Abdullah ibn Umar** and **Zayd ibn Thabit** (the latter also known for scribing the Uthmanic Mushaf). Their followers formed circles that emphasized strict adherence to the companions' traditions, especially about worship practices. Medina's school produced numerous transmitters focused on combining the outward correctness of recitation with a deeper spiritual etiquette (adab) during recitation sessions.

17.8.2 Mecca: Scholars of Ibn Abbas's Lineage

Mecca's scholarship drew heavily on **Ibn Abbas's** exegesis, refined by tabi'un like Mujahid, 'Ata' ibn Abi Rabah, and Ikrimah. They concentrated on explaining the historical contexts of revelation, reflective of Mecca's significance as the site of the earliest revelations. This tradition also influenced pilgrims from across the empire who visited Mecca, spreading the Meccan interpretive style to their homelands.

17.8.3 Iraq: Rivalry Between Kufa and Basra

Kufa and Basra, founded as garrison towns, developed vibrant scholarly scenes. Kufa was rooted in Ibn Mas'ud's readings, while Basra boasted grammarians like Sibawayh and exegetes like al-Hasan al-Basri. The friendly rivalry between these cities produced a robust variety of perspectives. Because they each laid claim to certain companions' legacies, travelers often moved between Basra and Kufa to compare teachings, fostering a rich environment of cross-pollination.

17.8.4 Syria and Egypt

Damascus inherited Uthmanic textual authority from the time of Muawiyah, while Fustat (in Egypt) integrated the teachings of companions who settled there, such as 'Amr ibn al-'As. In both regions, reciters taught recognized qira'at lines, and local scholars contributed smaller commentaries. By the Abbasid era, these areas, though overshadowed by Baghdad's ascendancy, still hosted teachers who traced their knowledge back to luminaries like Ibn 'Amir in Damascus or the circle of 'Abdullah ibn 'Amr ibn al-'As in Egypt.

17.9 Preservation of Scholarly Works

17.9.1 Oral Transmission and Early Writing

In the first two centuries, many scholarly remarks on the Quran were preserved orally. While some partial manuscripts existed, most systematic compilations appeared later, especially in the Abbasid period. For example, remarks by Mujahid or Qatadah might circulate among students in a chain of memorized commentary before being documented in full. This oral environment demanded that each generation ensure the chain's reliability.

17.9.2 Compilations by Later Authors

By the third and fourth centuries AH, major authors—al-Tabari, Ibn Abi Hatim, and others—sought out these older transmissions to create large, verse-by-verse compendia. They often quoted entire passages from the earlier masters verbatim. Through these later works, we can glimpse how scholars in the first century or two approached the Quran. Even if the earliest layers are now accessible only through references in extant tafsirs, the continuity of method and content reveals a remarkable fidelity to the initial interpretive tradition.

17.9.3 Influence on Subsequent Generations

The doctrines, interpretive principles, and recitation methods championed by these early scholars became normative for the ummah at large. Sunni orthodoxy, in particular, venerates the interpretive stances of Ibn Abbas, Ibn Mas'ud, and others as close to the Prophet's time. Shi'a scholarship likewise references Ali's teachings and the instructions of his family, often intersecting with the same textual tradition even if enriched by distinct theological emphases. Thus, the multi-faceted legacy of early Quranic scholars undergirded the entire edifice of future Islamic thought.

Chapter Eighteen: Transmission Across Regions and Cultures

18.1 Introduction

From the earliest days of Islam, the Quran's message traveled along trade routes, through conquest, and via personal journeys of scholars and pilgrims. By the time the Abbasid Caliphate reached its zenith, the faith had extended far beyond the Arabian Peninsula, finding new homes among Berbers in North Africa, Turks in Central Asia, Indians on the subcontinent, and later Malays in Southeast Asia. In each region, local populations engaged with the Quran—learning to recite it in Arabic, building mosques where it was taught, and eventually producing indigenous scholars who offered unique perspectives.

In this chapter, we explore the vast **geographical and cultural spread** of the Quran, from North Africa to East Asia. We will examine the **methods of teaching** that enabled non-Arabic speakers to grasp the text, the creation of **local calligraphic styles**, the interplay of **oral and written** forms of transmission, and the ways in which the **Quran shaped local customs**. By looking at how different societies absorbed and interacted with the Quranic revelation, we gain an appreciation for its role as a unifying scriptural foundation across a mosaic of languages and customs, while also seeing how diverse cultural influences enriched Islamic civilization as a whole.

18.2 Expansion into North Africa and Al-Andalus

18.2.1 Early Conquests and Berber Embrace of Islam

Muslim armies first entered North Africa under the Rashidun caliphs and continued pushing westward under the Umayyads. By the late 7th and early 8th centuries CE, large swathes of the Maghreb (modern-day Libya, Tunisia, Algeria, and Morocco) had come under nominal Islamic rule. Early on, Berber tribes embraced Islam in varying degrees—some purely for political reasons, others out of genuine conviction. As time went on, local acceptance deepened, with the Quran gradually integrated into Berber social life.

Quranic teachers accompanied the armies or arrived soon after to establish mosques and schools (kuttab). Although Berber languages remained strong in oral communication, the new faith anchored written literacy in Arabic. Over generations, a bilingual environment emerged, where educated Berbers read the Quran in Arabic while speaking Berber dialects at home. This dynamic facilitated the integration of Quranic values into local customs, fostering a sense of unity among diverse tribes.

18.2.2 The Rise of Qayrawan and Fez as Intellectual Centers

Cities like **Qayrawan** (in modern Tunisia) and **Fez** (in Morocco) became major hubs of Quranic scholarship. By the Abbasid era, local dynasties—such as the Aghlabids in Ifriqiya—sponsored mosques and madrasas where recitation and basic tafsir were taught. Over time, these centers produced scholars proficient in both Arabic linguistic sciences and local knowledge. They taught recognized qira'at (especially Warsh 'an Nafi' in North Africa), ensuring that the Uthmanic Mushaf's text remained consistent.

Fez, founded by Idris I (a descendant of Ali), eventually boasted one of the oldest universities in the world, al-Qarawiyyin, recognized for advanced religious studies. Students from across the Maghreb and even al-Andalus (Muslim Spain) attended classes on the Quran, grammar, law, and hadith, shaping a vibrant scholarly scene that thrived well into later centuries.

18.2.3 Al-Andalus and the Umayyad Emirate

When Umayyad forces crossed the Strait of Gibraltar in 711 CE, they established what became **al-Andalus** (Islamic Spain). Cordoba, Granada, and Seville emerged as cultural centers that blended Arabic-Islamic traditions with the region's Roman and Visigothic heritage. Quranic schools formed in mosques, and local scholars developed calligraphic styles known collectively as the **Maghribi script**, distinguished by looping forms and decorative flourishes.

Despite occasional political upheavals, al-Andalus produced illustrious Quranic scholars and reciters. The synergy of Arabic with local Romance dialects led to unique forms of poetry and literature. Knowledge of the Quran was widespread, forming a moral and cultural framework for a society that, at its peak, hosted remarkable achievements in philosophy, medicine, and architecture (epitomized by the Great Mosque of Cordoba, featuring Quranic inscriptions and majestic arches).

18.3 Movement into Sub-Saharan Africa

18.3.1 The Sahara as a Bridge

While North Africa was integrated into the broader Islamic world relatively early, **Sub-Saharan Africa** came to know the Quran largely through trans-Saharan trade routes. Traders carried not just salt, gold, and goods but also the message of Islam. Empires like Ghana, Mali, and Songhai eventually embraced Islam among their ruling elites, with the Quran playing a key role in legitimizing governance and linking these kingdoms to the global Islamic community.

18.3.2 Timbuktu and the Spread of Quranic Learning

Timbuktu, in the region of modern Mali, grew into a fabled center of Islamic scholarship from the 14th century onward. Merchants from North Africa and beyond established schools that taught reading, memorization, and basic tafsir. Manuscripts copied in Timbuktu's scriptoriums, often in the West African **Sudanic** or **Maghribi** scripts, circulated throughout the Sahel. The local tradition of copying and preserving Quranic texts persisted for centuries; indeed, many of these manuscripts still exist, offering insight into how Sub-Saharan communities internalized the Quran.

18.3.3 Cultural Synthesis and Oral Traditions

In much of West Africa, local communities fused Islamic practices with indigenous customs. Oral traditions—a hallmark of African cultures—blended seamlessly with the emphasis on **memorizing** the Quran. Scholars known as **ulama** or **marabouts** often introduced novices to short surahs, recited them in melodic chant, and accompanied them with moral teachings relevant to village life. Over time, this synergy nurtured robust Islamic institutions, where the Quran, while remaining in Arabic, shaped communal identity and moral codes.

18.4 The Quran's Journey East: Persia, Central Asia, and Beyond

18.4.1 Islamization of Persia

The conquest of the Sasanian Empire under the Rashidun and early Umayyads led to the gradual Islamization of Persia. As Persian speakers embraced Islam, they contributed significantly to the development of religious sciences. By the Abbasid era, major Persian families rose to prominence in Baghdad, championing advanced scholarship on the Quran's language and interpretation. While Arabic remained the liturgical language, new Persian converts wrote bilingual commentaries or glosses, helping co-religionists grasp basic Quranic vocabulary.

18.4.2 Central Asia and the Silk Road

Muslim rule extended into **Transoxiana** (modern Uzbekistan, Tajikistan) by the early 8th century. Cities like **Bukhara**, **Samarkand**, and **Khwarazm** became nodes where merchants, travelers, and scholars exchanged goods and knowledge. The Quran arrived with Arab settlers and missionaries, who built mosques and established recitation schools. Local Turkic and Persian populations gradually converted, typically learning enough Arabic to read the Quran's text while maintaining their native tongues.

Central Asia produced significant intellectual figures—like **Imam al-Bukhari** (d. 870 CE), famed for hadith scholarship—whose grounding in the Quran shaped their broader work. The region's status on the Silk Road meant travelers from China and India also encountered Islamic teachings, contributing to the Quran's global diffusion well beyond the borders of the caliphate.

18.4.3 Mongol Conquests and Legacy

Though the Mongols sacked Baghdad in 1258 CE, many Mongol rulers in Central Asia later embraced Islam, bringing the Quran into their courts. As Mongol dominions fractured into smaller khanates, each region continued the tradition of reading the Quran in Arabic, supporting local madrasas to teach recitation and exegesis. The Persian-influenced environment produced new commentaries and translations of the Quran's meanings into Persian for study purposes—though ritual recitation remained in Arabic.

18.5 The Quran in the Indian Subcontinent

18.5.1 Early Contacts via Trade and Umayyad Expeditions

Long before large-scale Muslim conquests, Arab traders frequented the coastal regions of Kerala and Gujarat in India, introducing local communities to Islamic beliefs. Small pockets of Muslims established themselves, building mosques where the Quran was recited. By 712 CE, an Umayyad military campaign under Muhammad ibn Qasim conquered parts of Sindh, planting a more visible Islamic presence. However, significant Islamic expansion in India would come in later centuries under various dynasties.

18.5.2 Sufi Orders and Quranic Devotion

From the 12th century onward, Sufi mystics played a pivotal role in spreading Islam throughout the subcontinent. Many Sufis brought well-worn Quranic manuscripts, reciting them daily in their lodges (khanqahs) and teaching novices the fundamentals of Arabic needed for worship. Their approach emphasized the Quran's spiritual message, focusing on personal purification and remembrance of God.

Sufi orders—like the Chishti, Suhrawardi, or Naqshbandi—often cultivated a deep reverence for the Quran, reciting selected passages in rhythmic liturgical ceremonies (majalis) to instill devotion. Over generations, local populations, impressed by the moral example of these Sufis, adopted the faith, learning enough Arabic to recite basic surahs. This spiritual approach to the Quran, more than direct conquest or official decree, fueled much of Islam's expansion across India.

18.5.3 Establishment of Madrasas and Commentaries

By the time of the Delhi Sultanate (13th–16th centuries) and later the Mughal Empire, numerous madrasas were founded. Students studied the Quran systematically, often with parallel instruction in Persian (the courtly language) and local vernaculars. Commentaries on the Quran, typically written in Arabic or Persian, circulated among the scholarly class. Some Mughal-era scholars even ventured to produce partial translations or paraphrases in local languages—though formal Arabic recitation was universally maintained for liturgical use. The synergy of Persian culture, local Indian traditions, and the universal authority of the Quran produced a rich tapestry of Islamic scholarship in the subcontinent.

18.6 Transmission into Southeast Asia and China

18.6.1 Maritime Trade and the Role of Merchants

Long before any military campaign, **merchant ships** sailing across the Indian Ocean carried the Quran's message to the Malay Archipelago (modern Indonesia, Malaysia, Brunei) and coastal pockets of the Philippines. Arab, Persian, and Indian Muslim traders settled in port cities like Malacca, Aceh, and Patani, establishing small communities that built mosques and taught the Quran. Over centuries, local rulers converted, encouraging their subjects to follow suit.

18.6.2 The Jawi and Pegon Scripts

While Arabic remained the standard for Quranic recitation, Southeast Asian Muslims developed modified scripts to write their own languages: **Jawi** (for Malay using Arabic characters) and **Pegon** (for Javanese or Sundanese, also using adapted Arabic script). Through these writing systems, religious teachers were able to produce simple texts explaining Quranic precepts in local tongues, bridging the linguistic gap without altering the original Arabic text used in worship.

18.6.3 China's Hui Muslims and the Quran

Islam reached China through both the Silk Road land routes and maritime avenues along China's southern coast. Hui Muslims (ethnically Chinese but practicing Islam) integrated the Quran into their religious life, reciting it in Arabic while sometimes reading Chinese commentaries or marginal notes. By the Ming and Qing dynasties, small centers of Islamic learning arose in Xi'an, Beijing, and Yunnan. These communities adapted Chinese calligraphic aesthetics to Arabic script in mosque decorations, creating unique Sino-Islamic art forms. The Quran's text thus remained identical but found itself in new cultural visual contexts, from traditional Chinese motifs to local architectural motifs.

18.7 Oral and Written Dimensions of Transmission

18.7.1 The Dominance of Oral Recitation

Across all these diverse regions—North Africa, Sub-Saharan Africa, the Indian subcontinent, Southeast Asia, and beyond—**oral recitation** remained the primary means by which the Quran was transmitted to the masses. The method of memorizing the text (hifz) endured as a hallmark of Islamic devotion. Many communities prized the title of **hafiz**, awarding it to those who recited the entire Quran from memory.

This reliance on oral learning provided continuity. Even if local conditions—climate, warfare, or limited resources—made written manuscripts scarce, the memorized text persisted. Teachers spent years drilling their students in accurate pronunciation, ensuring that local accents did not erode the integrity of the revealed words. This tradition created a global chain of continuous recitation, with every region effectively connected to the same scriptural source.

18.7.2 The Growing Role of Manuscripts

Simultaneously, as paper-making spread from the Middle East to other areas, more **written Mushafs** became available. Wealthy patrons endowed mosques with copies of the Quran. Rulers and local elites commissioned ornate manuscripts, sometimes with regional decorative styles. Over time, a synergy of oral and written modes developed: even though orality anchored communal memory, the presence of standardized codices in major mosques guaranteed reference points for settling disputes or verifying reciters' memories.

18.7.3 Local Calligraphic Innovations

In each cultural sphere, scribes blended classical Arabic scripts with local artistic motifs. For instance, in West Africa's Sahel region, manuscripts in **Sudani style** featured bold strokes and minimal diacritical marks, while in Ottoman realms, master calligraphers refined scripts like **Naskh** and **Thuluth** with swirling ornamentation. In all cases, scribes followed the same consonantal skeleton derived from the Uthmanic Mushaf, ensuring textual uniformity across far-flung lands.

18.8 Cultural Adaptations and the Quran's Universal Appeal

18.8.1 Language of Worship vs. Vernacular Expressions

One notable aspect of the Quran's transmission globally is the consistent retention of **Arabic** for liturgical recitation, considered essential to preserving the text's original form. At the same time, societies developed parallel traditions of explaining the Quran in local languages—through sermons, commentaries, or paraphrased translations known as **tafsir bil-lisan** (interpretation in the spoken tongue). This approach allowed believers to comprehend the moral and theological messages while upholding the primacy of the Arabic text in formal prayers and communal readings.

18.8.2 Integration into Local Festivities and Rituals

In many regions, reciting the Quran during life-cycle events (e.g., weddings, funerals, births) became a core cultural practice. Families would invite a hafiz to recite certain surahs for blessings. Communal gatherings in Ramadan often featured nightly tarawih prayers, where an entire recitation of the Quran was completed across the month. These customs reinforced the sense that the Quran was not a distant scripture but part of the daily texture of communal life.

18.8.3 Balancing Orthodoxy and Local Expressions

While the core text and essential religious obligations remained the same, localities often infused practices with indigenous cultural elements. The presence of **Sufism** encouraged spiritual and artistic expressions of Quranic devotion, such as melodic chanting (dhikr) or swirling dances (as with the whirling dervishes in the Turkish context). Orthodox scholars sometimes debated the propriety of such practices, yet the fundamental consensus that the Quran's text itself was inviolable served as a unifying anchor. Over centuries, this tension between local cultural expressions and scriptural orthodoxy shaped unique Islamic identities, all rooted in the same holy book.

18.9 Translation of the Quran's Meanings

18.9.1 Early Cautious Attitudes

From a traditional perspective, many Muslim scholars hesitated to produce full **translations** of the Quran's text, fearing that any rendering might lose the inimitable eloquence of the original Arabic. However, partial explanatory translations or paraphrases were permitted, especially for didactic purposes, so long as believers recognized these were **interpretations** rather than a substitute for the Arabic Mushaf.

18.9.2 Persian and Turkic Explanatory Renderings

Among the earliest translations emerged in **Persia**, where scholars wrote commentaries in Persian explaining each Arabic verse's meaning. Over time, these commentaries included line-by-line Persian glosses. Similarly, in Central Asia, some Turkic lines of interpretation emerged. These texts never replaced the Arabic recitation but helped non-Arabic speakers glean the Quran's essence.

18.9.3 Impact on Spread of Islamic Knowledge

Such explanatory works facilitated deeper assimilation of Quranic teachings in non-Arabic regions. Students could refer to a side-by-side Persian commentary while memorizing the Arabic text, thereby bridging linguistic gaps. Eventually, as Islam expanded globally (e.g., into the Malay world), translations or partial paraphrases in languages like Malay also appeared. The principle remained: the Arabic text was unaltered, but interpretive translations were welcomed for educational clarity, marking a pragmatic approach to diverse linguistic realities.

18.10 Challenges to Transmission and How They Were Overcome

18.10.1 Geographic Barriers

From the Sahara Desert to Himalayan passes, many regions faced logistical difficulties in acquiring manuscripts or hosting qualified teachers. Nevertheless, traveling scholars and merchants overcame these obstacles, often carrying sections of the Quran or entire Mushafs in caravans. They also trained local reciters who could continue teaching once the travelers departed. The portability of memorized scripture proved vital in bridging these remote locales.

18.10.2 Sectarian or Political Strife

In some areas, internal Muslim conflicts or local resistance to outside influence complicated the Quran's acceptance. For instance, certain tribes might retain pre-Islamic customs that clashed with Islamic norms. Yet over generations, once trust was established with local leaders or Sufi saints, the Quran's moral and spiritual appeal often won hearts. Even during sectarian clashes (e.g., between Sunni and Shi'a groups), the fundamental reverence for the same Book tempered the extent of potential rifts.

18.10.3 Environmental Factors

Humidity, heat, or insects threatened physical manuscripts in tropical climates. Communities improvised protective measures—like storing Mushafs in special wooden boxes or using materials more resistant to moisture. Oral memorization again offset manuscript fragility, ensuring that knowledge persisted even if a physical copy deteriorated. This synergy between physical and mental preservation became a hallmark of Islamic civilization's approach to safeguarding scripture.

18.11 Harmonizing Diversity Through the Quran

18.11.1 Core Unifier of Muslim Identity

For countless Muslim societies across continents, the Quran served as the spiritual axis that transcended local differences in language, ethnicity, or custom. A Muslim from Morocco and another from Indonesia might share little in cultural background, yet both recognized the **same** Arabic verses, recited the **same** surahs in prayer, and revered the **same** Mushaf. This universal bond shaped the concept of the ummah—a community bound by faith rather than mere geography.

18.11.2 Encouraging Intellectual Exchange

Due to the Quran's status, scholars from distant lands sought out centers like Mecca, Medina, Damascus, Baghdad, or later Cairo, to perfect their recitation or deepen tafsir knowledge. On returning home, they brought updated interpretations, commentaries, or new recitational nuances, thereby enriching local scholarship. This cyclical exchange turned the Islamic world into an intellectually networked realm, knit together by the shared pursuit of understanding divine revelation.

18.11.3 Fostering Tolerance and Adaptability

While Muslims maintained a strong sense of theological orthodoxy and textual integrity, the historical record shows remarkable adaptability in how the Quran was taught and contextualized among varied cultures. Practices like partial translations or local artistic forms (calligraphy, architecture) did not threaten the text's unity; instead, they amplified its accessibility. Thus, across the vast Islamic world, from the Atlantic coast to China's frontiers, communities found ways to harmonize local tradition with the universal message of the Quran.

Chapter Nineteen: Schools of Recitation and Early Commentaries

19.1 Introduction

From the moment the Quran began to spread beyond Arabia, reciters and scholars faced the challenge of teaching a sacred text to a diverse and expanding Muslim community. The revelations were complete, and the standard text established by Caliph Uthman had become universally recognized. Yet how were the Quran's words to be pronounced, and what exactly did they mean in context? In response to these questions, two major fields took shape during the first few centuries of Islam: **schools of recitation (qira'at)** and **Quranic commentaries (tafsir)**.

This chapter delves into the development of these two fields, showing how early Muslims preserved **multiple recitational variants** inherited from the Prophet's companions while ensuring that all remained consistent with the Uthmanic Mushaf. We also examine the rise of **early commentaries**, which integrated companion traditions, linguistic insights, and historical context to clarify obscure verses. By exploring these parallel evolutions—one focused on **how** to recite, the other on **how** to interpret—we see the deep commitment to safeguarding the Quran not just in its written form, but in its **phonetic** and **semantic** integrity. We also see how these specialized disciplines fostered the growth of a learned class of scholars, whose influence would extend far beyond scriptural study into law, theology, and the shaping of early Islamic society.

19.2 Emergence of Recognized Recitations

19.2.1 Reasons for Multiple Recitational Styles

From the very beginning of Islam, the Prophet Muhammad permitted certain dialectical variations for new Muslims who found the Qurayshi dialect challenging. This allowance was meant to facilitate ease of memorization and devotion. After the Prophet's death, the companions generally agreed to unify the text along the lines compiled by Uthman, yet **some** had learned from the Prophet using slightly different dialectal pronunciations or minor adjustments (e.g., elongating vowels, merging or separating certain words). These differences remained within permissible bounds—none altered the meaning of the text, but they reflected the reality of Arabia's linguistic diversity.

As Islam spread, prominent reciters in major cities like Medina, Mecca, Kufa, Basra, and Damascus each maintained a teaching lineage rooted in a particular companion's approach. Over time, the identity of these lineages solidified, especially once formal instruction demanded a recognized teacher with a **chain of transmission** (isnad) linking back to the Prophet.

19.2.2 The Uthmanic Standard and Local Practices

While the consonantal skeleton of every manuscript was uniform after Uthman's standardization, the **vowel markings** and **diacritical points** were initially minimal. This limited script left room for each region's recognized reciter to supply the correct vocalization. For instance, whether a short vowel was pronounced -u- or -a-, or whether a hamzah was lightly pronounced or more heavily enunciated, could vary in legitimate ways so long as the reading did not contradict the established text or Arabic grammar.

Many local communities grew accustomed to the style taught by a renowned reciter in their area, and these recitations began to be handed down meticulously. Teachers would recite an entire surah, students would echo it, and errors or divergences from the local "canonical" style were corrected on the spot. This environment fostered enormous respect for reciters who had spent years perfecting their craft, eventually earning the authority to teach others.

19.2.3 Toward Recognition of Multiple Qira'at

Initially, there might have been **numerous** local readings, some with uncertain chains of transmission or minor scribal influences. However, by the 2nd/8th and 3rd/9th centuries, recognized scholars of qira'at began distinguishing between authentic recitations (those demonstrably traced to the companions and conforming to the standard text) and unverified variations. Gradually, the community coalesced around a small number of "schools" whose reciters had impeccable reputations for precision and piety. These schools, each named for an **imam** of recitation, formed the bedrock of Quranic recitation across the empire.

19.3 The Major Schools of Recitation

19.3.1 The Seven Canonical Qira'at

One of the most pivotal developments was the work of **Abu Bakr ibn Mujahid** (d. 324 AH / 936 CE), who identified seven canonical reciters. This did not imply that all other recitations were invalid—some were recognized later, culminating in the well-known "Ten" or even "Fourteen" recitations across extended scholarship. Yet the "Seven" tradition gained enormous traction. These reciters, each from a central city of Islamic learning, included:

1. **Nafi' al-Madani** (d. 169 AH / 785 CE) in Medina
2. **Ibn Kathir al-Makki** (d. 120 AH / 737 CE) in Mecca
3. **Abu 'Amr ibn al-'Ala'** (d. 154 AH / 770 CE) in Basra
4. **Ibn 'Amir al-Dimashqi** (d. 118 AH / 736 CE) in Damascus
5. **Asim ibn Abi al-Nujud** (d. 127 AH / 745 CE) in Kufa
6. **Hamzah al-Zayyat** (d. 156 AH / 772 CE) in Kufa
7. **al-Kisa'i** (d. 189 AH / 805 CE), also in Kufa

Each of these reciters taught many students, among whom a few (termed **rawis**) became especially famous for transmitting the imam's method. For instance, the recitation of Asim became known primarily through the transmissions of **Hafs** and **Shu'bah**, with Hafs's version later dominating in many parts of the Muslim world.

19.3.2 Additional Recognized Reciters

Over time, scholars recognized three additional qira'at as canonical (making Ten in total). These included reciters like **Abu Ja'far al-Madani** in Medina, **Ya'qub al-Hadrami** in Basra, and **Khalaf** in Kufa. Despite being codified after the Seven, these qira'at met the same criteria: reliable chains of transmission, consistency with the Uthmanic text, and conformity to recognized norms of Arabic grammar.

19.3.3 Distinguishing Canonical from Shadh Readings

Any recitation that lacked a solid chain, contradicted the consonantal skeleton, or violated established linguistic principles was deemed **shadh** (irregular) and not permissible for liturgical use. While such readings might appear occasionally in scholarly works—often to illustrate linguistic possibilities—they carried no formal authority in worship. The "canonical" recitations thus represented a consensus approach, ensuring that even with variant details, all recognized qira'at shared a common textual core and revered lineage.

19.4 Methods and Significance of Qira'at Transmission

19.4.1 Intense Oral Training

Learning a canonical recitation required diligent practice under a qualified master. Pupils had to recite the entire Quran, usually multiple times, meticulously matching the teacher's pronunciation of each letter, vowel, and pause. The teacher corrected any slip, from slight misplacements of the tongue to timing of elongations. Only after mastering the reading to the teacher's satisfaction would a student receive **ijazah**—formal permission to teach others.

This system paralleled the **hadith** tradition of isnad: each reciter's chain traced back to the founding imam and ultimately to a companion or the Prophet. The atmosphere was reverential, as reciters believed they were preserving the exact phonetic form in which God's word had been revealed. Indeed, the very definition of "authentic" recitation hinged on unbroken chains of living practitioners.

19.4.2 Communal Identity Through Recitation

Different regions often adopted a particular recitation as standard for communal prayers. For instance, North Africa historically favored **Warsh 'an Nafi'** from Medina, while in large parts of the Middle East and beyond, **Hafs 'an 'Asim** prevailed. Local communities took pride in their recitational heritage. During Ramadan or major festivals, local imams would demonstrate their mastery of the region's canonical style, reinforcing cultural identity within the broader unity of the same Mushaf.

19.4.3 Safeguarding the Quranic Text

The existence of multiple recognized recitations did not lead to contradictory texts; rather, it **strengthened** the Quran's preservation by providing multiple vantage points on how to pronounce it. All canonical readings adhered to the Uthmanic consonantal skeleton, and none changed essential meanings. This synergy between orality and script gave the Muslim community a robust system of checks and balances: if a scribal error emerged in a manuscript, or if someone introduced a new reading without a valid chain, the well-established reciters would detect it immediately. Thus, these recitational schools were key guardians of the text's integrity.

19.5 Rise of Early Commentaries (Tafsir)

19.5.1 Origins of Tafsir

While recitation addressed **how** to pronounce the Quran, tafsir addressed **what** it meant. During the Prophet's lifetime, he explained verses as needed, clarifying obscure references. After his death, the companions continued these interpretations, each sometimes specializing in certain aspects (e.g., Ibn Abbas known for asbab al-nuzul, Ibn Mas'ud for linguistic nuances, Ubayy ibn Ka'b for theological points). Their students among the tabi'un then compiled or further elaborated on these teachings.

The earliest forms of tafsir were often short glosses—explanations of a verse's background or a single phrase's meaning—preserved in memory or rudimentary "notebooks." Over the next century, scholars seeking more systematic coverage began collecting these reports in verse-by-verse order, eventually producing coherent commentaries. The impetus for such thoroughness came partly from new converts lacking direct knowledge of Arabic or the Prophet's era; they needed guidance to fully appreciate the Quran's references and moral directives.

19.5.2 Key Sources for Early Tafsir

Early mufassirun (exegetes) drew on several categories of evidence:

1. **Companion Statements**: The most authoritative source. A chain of transmission (isnad) linking a commentary directly to Ibn Abbas, Ibn Umar, A'ishah, or Ali carried immense weight.
2. **Hadith of the Prophet**: Where the Prophet himself had explained a verse, that explanation was final and conclusive. Scholars scoured hadith compilations for any relevant verses.
3. **Asbab al-Nuzul** (circumstances of revelation): Knowledge of the historical event prompting a particular verse often clarified ambiguous language. For instance, references to specific battles or treaties showed how a verse addressed that moment.
4. **Arabic Linguistic Analysis**: Grammar, morphology, and pre-Islamic poetry references helped unravel complex phrases or idioms.
5. **Rational Reflection (Ra'y)**: While some scholars were cautious about personal opinions, certain aspects of the text—especially parables or universal moral teachings—invited reasoned interpretation. Mufassirun typically balanced rational insights with transmitted knowledge.

19.5.3 Tafsir Bi'l-Ma'thur vs. Tafsir Bi'l-Ra'y

Two broad methodologies crystallized:

- **Tafsir bi'l-ma'thur** (exegesis by transmitted reports): Emphasized direct reliance on the Prophet's and companions' statements, with minimal personal speculation.
- **Tafsir bi'l-ra'y** (exegesis by reasoned judgment): Allowed measured intellectual effort, including using grammatical, rhetorical, or theological reasoning to interpret verses not explicitly explained by companions or hadith.

Nevertheless, the boundary was not rigid. Many major commentators combined both, rooting their commentary in transmitted evidence but using rational arguments to elaborate on moral or theological dimensions. This synergy was especially evident in the Abbasid era, where advanced knowledge of Arabic grammar, literary style, and even philosophical concepts shaped interpretive approaches.

19.6 Notable Early Commentators and Their Contributions

19.6.1 Mujahid ibn Jabr (d. 104 AH / 722 CE)

A student of Ibn Abbas, **Mujahid** compiled a commentary that, while not fully surviving as a single volume, heavily influenced subsequent works. He recorded many of Ibn Abbas's direct statements, focusing on the literal sense of verses, historical contexts, and lexical clarifications. Mujahid refrained from elaborate theological speculation, preferring a more direct style. His approach exemplified a transitional phase from purely companion-based transmissions toward more structured exegesis.

19.6.2 Qatadah ibn Di'amah al-Sadusi (d. 117 AH / 735 CE)

Qatadah, based in Basra, was known for a broad knowledge that spanned hadith, history, and tafsir. His commentary integrated genealogical and historical details—particularly about prophets and earlier communities—giving readers a fuller backdrop for each Quranic story. Qatadah's lively style included moral lessons, urging believers to emulate the pious examples in biblical and pre-Islamic narratives. His transmissions appear frequently in later tafsir works, even though he never compiled them into a single authoritative volume.

19.6.3 Al-Tabari (d. 310 AH / 923 CE): The Great Synthesizer

Although from a slightly later period, **Muhammad ibn Jarir al-Tabari** is often deemed the culminating figure in early tafsir. His monumental **Jami' al-Bayan 'an Ta'wil Ay al-Qur'an** meticulously organized earlier reports verse by verse. Al-Tabari cited the transmissions of companions, tabi'un, and recognized scholars like Mujahid or Qatadah, evaluating their authenticity and reconciling conflicts. His commentary became the gold standard for all subsequent exegetes, preserving an enormous corpus of earlier tafsir traditions. Al-Tabari's methodical approach laid the blueprint: weigh different opinions, justify one with linguistic or hadith-based arguments, and note alternative readings when credible.

19.7 Approaches Within Early Tafsir

19.7.1 Legal (Fiqh) Emphasis

Some commentators, especially those from Kufa or Medina, approached the Quran with an eye toward extracting **legal rulings**. Verses on marriage, divorce, inheritance, financial transactions, and criminal punishments were analyzed meticulously, referencing the Prophet's practice (Sunnah) and companion opinions. Scholars in these circles effectively created "tafsir fiqhi," focusing on implementing the Quran's instructions in daily life. This method contributed to the formation of the classical Sunni madhhabs, as each school developed interpretive stances around key legal verses.

19.7.2 Theological (Kalam) Analysis

Another strand, especially visible under the Abbasids, engaged in theological interpretation—addressing God's attributes, predestination vs. free will, or the nature of the hereafter. While early commentaries seldom delved deeply into **kalam** controversies, they sometimes contained references to debates about anthropomorphic descriptions of God or the createdness of the Quran. For instance, a verse describing God's hand or throne might prompt explanations ensuring believers understood them in a manner consistent with mainstream theology, neither literalizing them in a corporeal sense nor denying them entirely.

19.7.3 Mystical and Ethical Insights

Although a fully elaborated Sufi tafsir tradition emerged in later centuries, early ascetics like Hasan al-Basri or Sufyan al-Thawri occasionally offered spiritual reflections on verses. They might highlight a moral dimension, urging repentance, humility, or love of God. This "mystical-ethical" reading, while not yet a formal discipline, foreshadowed the more expansive Sufi commentaries that would arise, in which every verse was read for hidden spiritual layers guiding the soul's journey to God.

19.8 Interplay Between Qira'at and Tafsir

19.8.1 Variant Readings Yield Interpretive Nuances

Since recognized qira'at sometimes differed in small ways—such as whether a verb was in the active or passive voice—exegetes often noted how these differences could subtly shift the shade of meaning. For example, one reading might emphasize God's action upon a people, while another might highlight the people's own deed. Both were deemed valid but could produce distinct homiletic lessons. Early commentators recognized these variants as an enrichment of the text's interpretive richness, as long as each was anchored in a canonical recitation.

19.8.2 Using Recitation to Clarify Ambiguities

In certain verses, the Uthmanic script might allow more than one voweling if no explicit companion statement forbade it. Exegetes would check whether a known reciter had a definitive way of reading it. If so, they might adopt that reading in their commentary. Conversely, some exegetes used grammar-based arguments to champion one recitation variant over another. This reciprocal relationship between qira'at and tafsir ensured consistency while respecting legitimate diversity.

19.9 Preservation and Dissemination of Scholarly Works

19.9.1 Oral Circles and Written Transcripts

In early centuries, both recitation lineages and tafsir teachings were predominantly transmitted orally. Scholars might keep private notes, but formal "publishing" was limited. Pupils memorized entire commentaries or wrote them down in partial form. As paper-making advanced in the Abbasid era, more comprehensive works like al-Tabari's multi-volume commentary became feasible. Copyists in major cities reproduced popular tafsirs, distributing them across the empire's madrasas and libraries.

19.9.2 Madrasa Networks and Scholarly Exchange

By the 4th/10th century, the institution of the **madrasa** blossomed, providing a structured setting for advanced study of the Quran and its commentaries. Students traveled regionally to sit with revered masters, expanding the interplay of local recitational styles and exegesis traditions. This cross-pollination allowed, for instance, a Persian student in Nishapur to bring Kufa's qira'at to a teacher in Damascus, or a scholar from Fez to incorporate Basran grammatical insights into his commentary. The result was an increasingly cohesive world of Quranic scholarship, transcending linguistic and geographic borders.

19.9.3 The Role of Patronage

Wealthy patrons—caliphs, governors, or private notables—often sponsored the copying of major tafsirs or invited renowned reciters to their courts. While some rulers had political motives, the net effect was beneficial for scholarship: it ensured that knowledge circulated widely. For example, if a sultan built a large madrasa and endowed it with a library, he might procure copies of major tafsirs from Baghdad, Kufa, or Mecca, assembling them for local students to consult. Over time, these patron-supported centers became repositories of the Islamic community's collective interpretive wisdom.

19.10 Challenges and Debates in Early Scholarship

19.10.1 Debates Over Figurative vs. Literal Interpretation

One recurring tension was whether certain verses—particularly those describing the attributes of God or eschatological events—should be taken literally or figuratively. Scholars inclined to textual literalism (like the Zahiris) insisted on the plain sense unless proven otherwise, while more rational-minded exegetes permitted metaphorical readings if consistent with Arabic rhetorical norms. While these differences sometimes sparked heated debates, the shared acceptance of the same baseline text tempered divisiveness, ensuring all parties recognized the overarching sanctity of the Quran.

19.10.2 Grappling with "Allegorical" Verses

Verses deemed **mutashabihat** (ambiguous) posed special challenges. Examples include those about the nature of the soul, the unseen realms, or cryptic letters at the start of certain surahs (the **mysterious "Muqatta'at"**). Some exegetes took a cautious approach, acknowledging the limit of human comprehension and leaving the meaning to God (tafwid). Others ventured speculative interpretations, often referencing biblical lore (isra'iliyat) or adopting philosophical or mystical frameworks. The result was a spectrum of positions, showcasing the text's capacity to engage diverse intellectual energies without losing unity of purpose.

19.10.3 Controversies Over Weak Narrations

As the science of hadith criticism matured, exegetes sometimes discovered that a so-called "companion statement" or "Prophetic explanation" was poorly attested. Diligent scholars removed or flagged such weak reports, striving to keep tafsir free of spurious tales or improbable historical anecdotes. This vigilant cleansing process continued over centuries, with each generation refining the textual record. While some popular commentaries retained questionable stories for rhetorical effect, mainstream scholarship prioritized verifying each chain's authenticity.

19.11 Influence of Early Schools on Later Developments

19.11.1 Establishing Norms for Quranic Study

The early centuries laid down the structural norms of qira'at, commentary, grammar, and hadith. By the 5th/11th century, these disciplines were well-defined in scholarly curricula. Students typically began with memorizing the Quran and mastering one canonical recitation, then proceeded to read a classical tafsir—often al-Tabari or a slightly later commentary. Grammar treatises, such as Sibawayh's Al-Kitab, were mandatory for advanced interpretation. This layered approach remains influential in traditional Islamic seminaries even today (in the historical sense).

19.11.2 Bridging Geographical and Sectarian Divides

Despite political rivalries—Umayyads vs. Abbasids, or local dynasties in North Africa vs. the central caliphate in Baghdad—the foundational works of qira'at and tafsir circulated widely. Sunni and Shi'a communities alike referenced the same companion-based exegeses in many respects, though Shi'a scholarship might highlight Ali's statements or the Imams' commentaries more prominently. Because the Quran itself was undisputed, scholarship around it functioned as a broad corridor linking disparate corners of the Islamic world.

19.11.3 Setting the Stage for Medieval and Post-Classical Commentators

By the time later commentators like **al-Zamakhshari** (d. 538 AH / 1144 CE), **Fakhr al-Din al-Razi** (d. 606 AH / 1210 CE), or **Ibn Kathir** (d. 774 AH / 1373 CE) wrote their works, the early schools of recitation and exegesis were firmly established. These medieval scholars frequently cited the opinions and transmissions from earlier figures—Mujahid, Qatadah, al-Tabari—while adding more advanced rhetorical, theological, or legal insights. Indeed, one cannot fully appreciate classical or later tafsir without recognizing the foundation laid by the early masters who shaped the structure and methodology of Quranic study.

Chapter Twenty: Lasting Legacy in Early Islamic History

20.1 Introduction

Throughout the preceding chapters, we have traced the Quran's journey from its revelation in 7th-century Arabia to its widespread acceptance and study across a vast empire. We have explored how it was meticulously compiled, memorized, recited in canonical forms, and interpreted through scholarly commentary. Now, as we bring our narrative to a close, it is crucial to reflect on the **enduring impact** the Quran had on every facet of early Islamic civilization—shaping law, social norms, literary culture, spiritual life, and the very conception of a unified ummah (community).

This concluding chapter highlights the **long-term influences** the Quran exerted on early Islamic history. We will see how it served as **the ultimate reference** for moral conduct, inspired **scholarly and cultural** developments, and provided a **rallying point** for Muslim identity across ethnic, linguistic, and geographic boundaries. By appreciating the scale of this legacy, we recognize how the Quran was not just a text recited in worship; it was a **foundational constitution**, a **spiritual guide**, and a **cultural beacon** that left an indelible mark on the formative centuries of the Muslim world.

20.2 The Quran as a Unifying Scripture

20.2.1 Bridging Tribal and Cultural Differences

In the Arabian Peninsula of the Prophet's time, tribes were notoriously fractious. The Quran's message of **tawhid** (the oneness of God) transcended the loyalties of clan and kinship, forging a community based on belief rather than lineage. As Islam spread into Syria, Iraq, Egypt, Persia, and beyond, local customs and languages varied widely. Yet the same **Arabic Mushaf** was held in reverence by all. This shared text acted as a unifying force, offering a **common language of**

devotion even among believers who otherwise spoke Berber, Persian, Greek, or other tongues at home.

20.2.2 Foundation for the Ummah

The concept of the ummah emerged from Quranic verses that called believers "one community" (Quran 21:92). Early caliphs referenced such verses to encourage unity in matters of governance and public welfare. Meanwhile, everyday Muslims derived from the Quran's injunctions a sense of fraternity across ethnic lines. This unity, rooted in the text, was not merely theoretical: it manifested in shared festivals, gatherings for tarawih prayers during Ramadan, pilgrimages where reciters from varied regions joined in the same surahs, and universal acceptance of the Uthmanic standard. In an era of frequent political strife, the Quranic ideal of unity consistently reminded believers of their deeper bonds.

20.2.3 Minimizing Scriptural Schism

While other faith traditions occasionally experienced significant textual disagreements leading to separate canons, the Muslim world, guided by the early compilation and canonical recitations, avoided major scriptural schisms. Whatever theological or political differences arose—Kharijite, Shi'a, Mu'tazilite—their adherents still turned to the **same** Arabic Quran. Even the recognized variant qira'at remained under a single textual umbrella. This phenomenon, rare in religious history, lent the Islamic community a textual stability that greatly influenced its trajectory through subsequent centuries.

20.3 Influence on Social Norms and Legal Systems

20.3.1 Quranic Ethics in Daily Conduct

From the earliest revelations, the Quran addressed ethical behavior: compassion for the poor, honesty in trade, fair dealings in marriage, and the rights of orphans. As Islamic rule spread, these injunctions provided broad guidance for social norms. In local markets, vendors were cautioned against cheating by verses condemning fraud (Quran 83:1–5). Families structured inheritance around explicit Quranic formulas (Quran 4:11–12). Even treatment of prisoners or slaves was informed by verses urging kindness and redemption. These moral directives proved adaptable across cultural frontiers, offering a core set of values that shaped personal and communal life.

20.3.2 Legal Codification in Fiqh

While the Quran did not present a fully systematic legal code, numerous verses formed the backbone of **fiqh** (Islamic jurisprudence). By referencing verses about contracts, criminal punishments, or marital obligations, jurists devised a sophisticated legal framework. Schools of law (Hanafi, Maliki, Shafi'i, Hanbali, and others) all championed the principle that **no** legal ruling could stand if it clearly contradicted the Quran. Under the Rashidun and Umayyad caliphs, Qadis (judges) used the Quran to resolve disputes. The Abbasid period saw further elaboration, with major compendia of jurisprudence frequently citing Quranic verses as **primary evidence** alongside Prophetic hadith.

20.3.3 Debate Over Interpretation

Yet the Quran's concise wording sometimes led to debates on application. For instance, if the Quran said "cut off the hand of the thief" (Quran 5:38), how severe should the theft be to warrant this punishment? Should the environment (e.g., famine) matter? Scholars parted ways on details, but none doubted the **binding authority** of the verse itself. The multiplicity of legal schools thus revealed the text's interpretive elasticity while underscoring its supreme authority as the legislative anchor for early Muslim societies.

20.4 Cultural and Artistic Expressions

20.4.1 Quranic Inspiration in Architecture

The building of mosques became a central expression of Islamic society, and the **Quran** was integral to their design. Architecture often featured inscriptions of key verses—like the "Throne Verse" (Quran 2:255) or passages emphasizing God's transcendence. Domes, minarets, and arches served as symbolic spaces for recitation. Structures like the **Dome of the Rock** in Jerusalem and the Great

Mosque of Damascus famously integrated large epigraphic panels, turning the Quran into a **visual** as well as **auditory** presence in public religious life.

20.4.2 Emergence of Calligraphic Traditions

Because figurative art in religious contexts was discouraged, Muslim artists funneled creative energy into **calligraphy**, elevating script to a revered art form. Copying the Quran became a prime demonstration of calligraphic skill. Early Kufic manuscripts were bold and majestic; later, more cursive forms like Naskh and Thuluth emerged under Abbasid patronage. Illuminated Qurans, adorned with gold leaf and geometric motifs, became prized possessions of rulers and elites. The reverence for the text and the avoidance of images catalyzed a distinct Islamic aesthetic that left a mark on manuscripts, architecture, and decorative arts.

20.4.3 Poetry and Literature

Though the Quran overshadowed pre-Islamic poetry's cultural dominance, it did not eliminate it. Instead, Muslim poets invoked **Quranic themes**—monotheism, moral reflection, stories of prophets—within their compositions. Writers in Arabic, Persian, and other languages alluded to verses, sometimes weaving them into panegyrics or mystical poetry. The interplay of scriptural references in classical Islamic literature gave these works a spiritual resonance and offered an ongoing demonstration of how deeply the Quran had permeated the literary imagination.

20.5 Language Development and Arabic Identity

20.5.1 Arabic as the Lingua Franca

Before Islam, Arabic was primarily the language of the Arabian Peninsula. Under the Rashidun and Umayyads, it became the administrative tongue of a vast empire, and under the Abbasids, it morphed into a sophisticated medium for science, philosophy, and literature. The **Quran** anchored this transformation, serving as the model of perfect Arabic. As new regions entered the Islamic fold, local elites learned Arabic to read the Quran, contributing to a broad-scale linguistic unification. Even after Persian, Turkish, or other languages rose in prestige, Arabic retained its unmatched status for religious matters.

20.5.2 Grammar and Lexicography

Because reading the Quran accurately was paramount, scholars like Sibawayh, al-Khalil ibn Ahmad, and others developed advanced grammar and lexicographic works. These not only safeguarded correct recitation but also laid the foundation for Arabic as a scholarly language. Over the centuries, Arabic grammar and philology thrived in madrasa curricula, ensuring that future generations could interpret the Quran with clarity. This heightened linguistic awareness also influenced how scribes approached other works of literature, strengthening Arabic's role as a refined scholarly medium.

20.5.3 Regional Languages and the Quran

While Arabic was the official language of worship, countless Muslim communities retained their local tongues for daily life. Yet the prestige of the Quranic text often spurred them to adopt modified Arabic scripts (e.g., Jawi in Southeast Asia, Ajami in parts of Africa) or incorporate Arabic loanwords for religious concepts. This interplay between Arabic and vernaculars enriched both domains: local languages gained new terminologies, and Arabic served as a unifying thread ensuring standard worship practices.

20.6 Shaping Political Legitimacy and Governance

20.6.1 Invocation of Quranic Authority by Caliphs

From the Rashidun era forward, rulers frequently cited the Quran to justify or frame their policies. While some, like the Umayyads, faced criticism for politicizing religion, the principle remained: no caliph could openly disregard or contradict the Quran without risking major unrest. This dynamic fostered an environment where caliphs had to position themselves as **protectors** of the scripture, commissioning mosque building, promoting recitation circles, and funding scholarship. In turn, the moral teachings of the Quran set certain boundaries for governance.

20.6.2 Legal Institutions and the "Quranic Court"

Judicial systems under early Islam emphasized the Qadi's reliance on the Quran. Though judges also used hadith and legal reasoning, the final reference always circled back to the text's verses when addressing key matters like inheritance shares, punishments for theft or slander, or rules about marriage and divorce. Over time, as the caliphate's authority became symbolic, local dynasties or sultanates still upheld the ideal that true legitimacy derived from ruling in accordance with **shari'ah**, the broad legal system anchored in the Quran.

20.6.3 Check on Rulers and Elites

Conversely, the Quran could serve as a **check** against tyrannical or irreligious behavior by rulers. Many a pious scholar invoked verses condemning oppression or injustice, challenging governors who levied excessive taxes or harmed citizens. While political realities were often complex, the moral force of the Quran was undeniable. Figures like Umar ibn Abdul Aziz (an Umayyad caliph famed for piety) actively reformed taxation and social policies to align more closely with Quranic principles. Though not always successful, these attempts reveal the text's role as an ethical yardstick for governance.

20.7 Spiritual Dimensions and Personal Devotion

20.7.1 Quranic Recitation as Worship

Beyond formal legal or social functions, the Quran was at the heart of **personal devotion**. Muslims recited verses for solace, reflection, or healing. The Prophet's example of night prayers (tahajjud) became common among ascetic circles, who would stand long hours reciting. Hasan al-Basri and later Sufi figures extolled the spiritual fruits of **deep reflection (tadabbur)** on each verse. As a result, many lay Muslims, even if they did not master advanced commentary, learned to recite selected surahs for daily prayers and spiritual nourishment, forging an intimate bond with the text.

20.7.2 Emergence of Hifz Culture

Memorizing the entire Quran (hifz) emerged as a special pursuit that conferred high esteem. A **hafiz** could lead prayers and was often seen as a moral role model. Some families dedicated resources to sending their children to study circles where memorization was systematically taught. Over time, entire lineages of scholars prided themselves on producing generation after generation of hafiz. This deep embedding of the Quran in personal memory made the text a living presence in countless Muslim homes and gatherings.

20.7.3 Sufi Traditions of Esoteric Reflection

While mainstream Sunni and Shi'a scholarship stressed the Quran's clear guidance, certain Sufi orders sought deeper, esoteric layers behind the literal words. They meditated on symbolic meanings, sometimes connecting the text to an inward journey of the soul. Even so, they upheld the same outward text recognized by the ummah. This tension between a literal-linguistic reading and a mystical-intuitive approach did not undermine the unity of the text; rather, it expanded the ways believers experienced the Quran's spiritual potency.

20.8 Quran and Interfaith Encounters

20.8.1 Relations with People of the Book

From the start, the Quran acknowledged **Jews and Christians** as "People of the Book," referencing the lineage of earlier prophets. Early Islamic governance, especially under the Rashidun and Umayyads, established dhimmi (protected) status for these communities. While the exact legal rights varied over time, the notion that Jews and Christians shared aspects of revealed scripture encouraged certain levels of coexistence. **Interfaith debates** in the Umayyad and Abbasid courts often hinged on biblical verses vs. Quranic verses, highlighting the text's significance as a reference point in dialogues with other monotheists.

20.8.2 Philosophical Exchanges in Abbasid Baghdad

Under the Abbasids, Baghdad became a crossroads where Greek, Persian, and Indian philosophical works were translated into Arabic. Muslim thinkers engaged with these ideas, often framing them in light of Quranic concepts. For instance, rationalist Mu'tazilites argued that the Quran pointed to a just God, consistent with reason, while more traditional theologians used verses to critique certain Hellenistic notions. Although these debates sometimes grew contentious, they showcased how the Quran functioned as **the** anchor for Islamic intellectual identity, even amid robust external influences.

20.8.3 Christians and Jews Studying Arabic

In Christian-majority regions later conquered by Muslims—such as Syria or parts of al-Andalus—some local Christians learned Arabic and engaged with the Quran to better understand Muslim neighbors. While many Christian theologians rejected Islamic revelation, they recognized the practical need to discuss theological differences using a shared vocabulary. A few even quoted Quranic passages in their polemics or theological treatises, indicating the text's widespread familiarity in early medieval Middle Eastern societies.

20.9 Summation of the Historical Arc

20.9.1 From Revelation to Empire

The Quran's journey began in the solitary cave of Hira with revelations to the Prophet Muhammad, forging a small community in Mecca and then Medina. Under the Prophet's leadership, the nascent ummah faced trials of persecution, migration, and battles, yet emerged with a robust moral code anchored in the Quran. The subsequent caliphs oversaw the text's compilation, standardization, and initial distribution.

20.9.2 Generations of Scholars and Institutions

Over the next centuries, as the Islamic empire spread from the Iberian Peninsula to Central Asia and beyond, the Quran guided governance and inspired countless believers. Scholars devoted themselves to perfecting its recitation (qira'at) and unveiling its meanings (tafsir). Their efforts resulted in canons of knowledge—grammatical treatises, legal manuals, exegetical works, and more—that enriched the entire civilization. By the Abbasid golden age, a complex but cohesive educational system formed, with the Quran at its apex.

20.9.3 Dissemination to Far Corners of the World

Merchants, pilgrims, and Sufi preachers carried the Quran's message across deserts, seas, and mountain passes, weaving it into the fabric of societies in Africa, Asia, and beyond. Overcoming linguistic barriers and diverse cultural norms, the Quran's universal call to monotheism and justice resonated widely. Local calligraphy and translations of its meanings further integrated it into each region's cultural tapestry, while reciters preserved the original Arabic text.

Conclusion of Chapter Twenty

In the early centuries of Islamic history, the Quran was not merely a holy text confined to ritual recitation; it served as the heartbeat of a civilization. It unified disparate tribes and nations under a shared creed, shaped moral and legal systems, inspired artistic and literary achievements, and created a transcontinental network of scholars bound by devotion to preserving the divine word. Its **linguistic excellence** propelled advancements in Arabic grammar, while its **moral directives** guided daily life and governance. At the same time, the text's **spiritual depth** spoke to mystics and theologians, fueling centuries of reflection and debate.

From the vantage point of these first few centuries, we see how the Quran's enduring influence was made possible by dedicated companions, scribes, reciters, and exegetes who safeguarded its textual and oral integrity. They built a tradition that balanced **strict authenticity** with **intellectual openness**, allowing the Quran to remain relevant in vastly different lands and times. Although political fortunes rose and fell—Rashidun unity giving way to Umayyad rule, then to the Abbasids, and eventually to a mosaic of sultanates—the Quran itself stayed **constant**, recognized as the unaltered word of God revealed in Arabic.

Thus, the **lasting legacy** of the Quran in early Islamic history is one of unity, creativity, and steadfast commitment. It spurred the formation of scholarly fields that ensured its correct recitation, thorough explanation, and integration into law and culture. This legacy laid the groundwork for Islam's further expansion and the dynamic civilizations that would arise in the medieval and early modern periods, all of which looked back to the same scripture that had guided the Prophet Muhammad and his companions centuries before. In summing up these early centuries, we see how the Quran shaped a faith, a community, and ultimately a broad-reaching civilization whose reverence for the divine word remains central to Islamic life even today (in historical perspective).

With these twenty chapters, we have traced the Quran's path from pre-Islamic Arabia to its firm establishment as the center of a global religious community. While our account stops here—at the dawn of Islam's medieval transformations—its story continues through later centuries of commentary, calligraphic brilliance, mystical insight, and intellectual endeavor. Yet the foundational narrative stands complete: from revelation and compilation, through expansions and scholarly elaborations, the Quran's **complete history** in the formative era stands as a testament to human devotion in service of divine revelation.

Help Us Share Your Thoughts!

Dear reader,

Thank you for spending your time with this book. We hope it brought you enjoyment and a few new ideas to think about. If there was anything that didn't work for you, or if you have suggestions on how we can improve, please let us know at **kontakt@skriuwer.com**. Your feedback means a lot to us and helps us make our books even better.

If you enjoyed this book, we would be very grateful if you left a review on the site where you purchased it. Your review not only helps other readers find our books, but also encourages us to keep creating more stories and materials that you'll love.

By choosing Skriuwer, you're also supporting **Frisian**—a minority language mainly spoken in the northern Netherlands. Although **Frisian** has a rich history, the number of speakers is shrinking, and it's at risk of dying out. Your purchase helps fund resources to preserve and promote this language, such as educational programs and learning tools. If you'd like to learn more about Frisian or even start learning it yourself, please visit **www.learnfrisian.com**.

Thank you for being part of our community. We look forward to sharing more books with you in the future.

Warm regards,
The Skriuwer Team

www.ingramcontent.com/pod-product-compliance
Lightning Source LLC
LaVergne TN
LVHW012045070526
838202LV00056B/5598